Leo Boatman, age 13, the first day of six years of brutal juvenile incarceration

BORN AND RAISED TO MURDER

A Failure of Foster Care

IRENE SULLIVAN,
RETIRED JUVENILE JUDGE

atmosphere press

To Ken Wooden:
Good friend, champion of children like
Leo Boatman, investigative reporter and author of
Weeping in the Playtime of Others. America's Incarcerated Children

Contents

PART 3

PART 4
Death Penalty Proceedings

PART 5
Letters from Leo

Author's Note

Indeed, Leo Boatman's life got off to a rough start.

Born in a mental hospital to a mother whose mental illness and drug addictions later caused her death, he and his older sister were raised by a loving grandmother. Leo excelled at school, impressing his teachers with his love of learning and reading books. He had behavior problems, but they were appropriately addressed by social workers and therapists who worked with the family.

When Leo's grandmother died, Leo was placed into a foster home run by an experienced married couple who were well trained in raising boys with family challenges in a caring, therapeutic environment, including nourishing meals, healthy athletic activities and help with homework.

When Leo graduated from high school and aged out of foster care, he received a full college scholarship from the state, as well as a monthly stipend for expenses. Leo's goal was to become a veterinarian, so he got a part-time job at an animal hospital and enrolled at a local college to begin training as a vet tech. Leo's foster parents considered him part of the family who should live with them while in college. Leo was grateful and insisted on paying them rent from money he earned from his part-time job.

Leo graduated from college with high honors and a full scholarship to the University of Florida's Veterinarian School. He lived on campus and worked part time at a local animal hospital. Grateful for the various forms of support that had enabled him to get to this point, Leo wanted to give back. He connected with foster children in the Gainesville area and arranged for them to volunteer at the animal hospital.

When Leo graduated from vet school, he applied for and received a grant from the Department of Children and Families to open his own veterinarian practice, which would employ foster children part time to teach them to care for needy animals. The foster children became known as Leo's Lions, and the program received national attention, including features on *60 Minutes* and the *Today Show*. Leo met a lovely woman who produced and filmed documentaries. They collaborated on one about Leo's Lions. They married and produced two "cubs" of their own, while continuing to run the animal hospital and employ foster children.

Tragically none of this is true: It is all what might have been, given Leo's very real love of learning and glimpses of his care about his fellow man, had the State of Florida not miserably failed him in every aspect of his life. Read on, please, to see how this failure to support the life, welfare and potential of a needy child predictably, inevitably and needlessly resulted in the tragic loss of many lives.

Prologue

January 2006

Towering pine trees. Fresh air. Needles crunching underfoot. Birdsong. Breeze. Bright sunlight. Leo inhaled deeply. So many sensations overwhelmed him. He hadn't felt them for six long years. Six years of prison bars, smelly cells, crap for food and snarling guards. The guards...the guards...the guards. He couldn't get them out of his head.

Camping in the Ocala National Park was a great idea. He'd unrolled his new sleeping bag at the park entrance the night before, slept under the stars and was the first one in when it opened at sunrise. He was looking forward to the adventure. He carried a week's worth of food and water in his backpack. The rifle slung over his shoulder would bag a squirrel or a rabbit if he ran out. Uncle Vic wouldn't miss the rifle.

He followed the compass directions uphill to Hidden Pond. It was beautiful, almost midday now. Warm for January. That's when he first saw them. A young couple, walking around the pond. The man had his arm around the woman's shoulders. They were laughing. Their tent poked up behind them. Leo decided his voice would be less startling than simply appearing in front of them.

"Hi there. Looks like you picked a great campsite. I'm going on a ways. I wonder if you could give me some directions." They both smiled at him. They weren't afraid. *The guards should see me now,* he thought. *Damn guards...get out of my mind.*

Leo guessed they were boyfriend and girlfriend, maybe

lovers, a few years older than he was. Lucky them. The man told him the way to the next good campsite. Leo climbed halfway up the short hill, sat down, knees bent, and watched them break camp. He could hear them laughing, teasing each other about the work and the breakfast. He was 19 and had never laughed easily with any girl or woman. He'd never even had a relationship. He'd been locked up since he was 13. Just guards… guards…guards. Damn fucking, foul-mouthed, mean and cruel guards. *Get the Hell out of this forest. Get out of my mind, guards. Get out of my body. You're making me so Goddamned mad…I don't know what I will do.*

Leo unshouldered the rifle and took aim. First at a tall pine, then at a scurrying squirrel, then at the campers. He steadied the rifle on his right knee. He was so angry. He wished he had a guard to kill. All of them. Here, just campers. He pointed the rifle at the kneeling, smiling man. As the man stood up, Leo pulled the trigger. The gunshot broke the silence and the man fell to the ground. The girl screamed. Leo aimed again and took her out too.

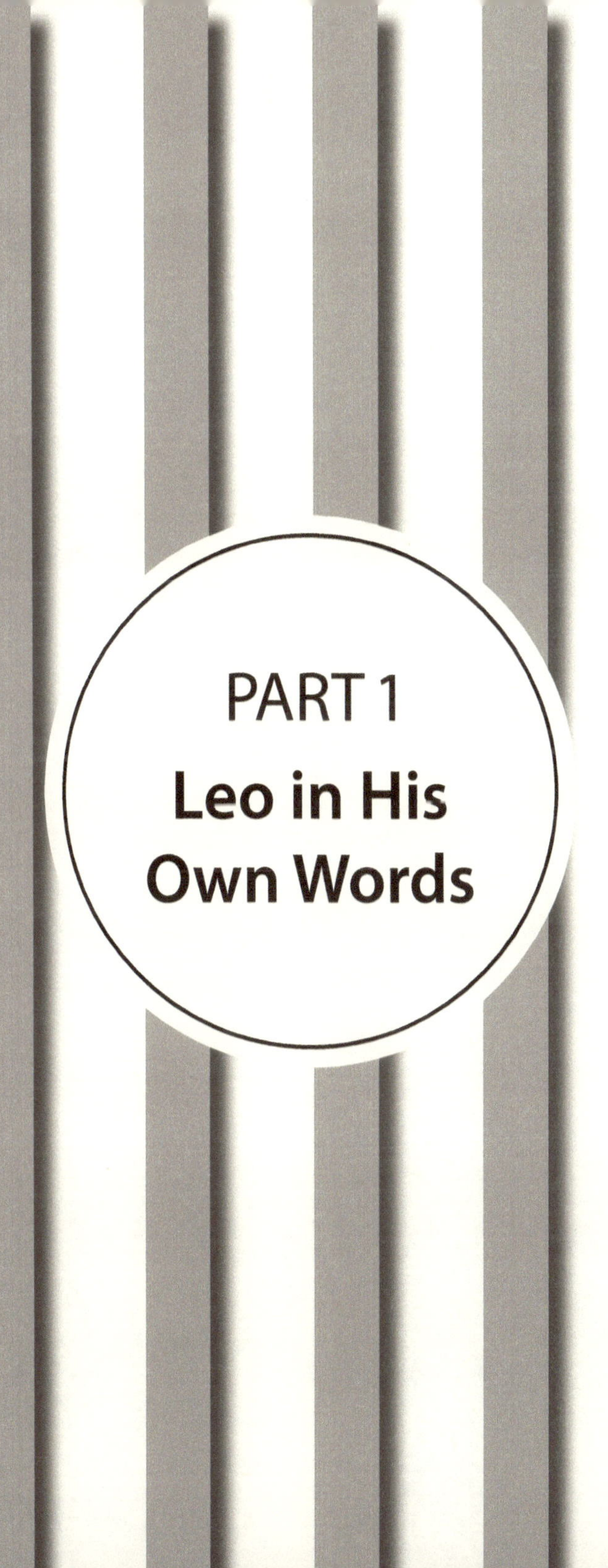
PART 1
Leo in His
Own Words

Chapter 1

My Birth
July 20, 1986

"Men and drugs, drugs and men. That's all your mother thinks about," my grandmother Lucille would tell my sister Rosie and me after throwing my mother and her current boyfriend out of the house again.

About my father, she was more evasive. "Don't ask about him," she'd say, or "I don't want to talk about him." As I got older, she'd say, "Your mother doesn't even know who he is. How would I know?"

I never asked my mother during the times she lived with us. I guess I was too embarrassed, even at an early age, or maybe I was afraid of the answer. I knew who Rosie's father was. I'd seen pictures of him. He was from Sri Lanka, which explained her darker skin. I hated Rosie then for having pictures of her father.

I pestered my mother's youngest brother, Vic, about my father so often that he finally made my grandmother tell me.

"Sheila quit high school and was constantly running away from home. I got sick of filing missing person's reports, but I always did. She'd find a man somewhere, live with him awhile till he hit her or threw her out, and she'd come dragging home. Again and again. Over and over.

"Well, one day after she'd been gone for months, we got a call from a mental hospital in Arcadia, Florida, about three hours away. Wouldn't you know that Sheila got herself admitted there some time before and didn't tell us. The reason they called was she'd gotten herself pregnant while there, and they wanted to know what to do about the baby, about you.

"I drove down to see her. She actually looked better, but she was taking all kinds of medication. She told me she was raped, either by another patient or a guard. She wouldn't identify him. If she knew who he was, she died without telling anyone. So, you were conceived and born in a mental hospital. No one knows who your father is and don't ask me about it again."

I wish I hadn't asked.

Can you guess how many times in life you have to write down your father's name or answer questions about him? "Unknown...unknown...unknown..." Talk about three strikes against you. Conceived *and* born in a mental hospital *and* father unknown.

The irony in my case is that the mental hospital later became DeSoto Correctional Institution for delinquent kids, one of the few "reform schools," or juvenile prisons the State *didn't* put me in during my six years behind bars. I was locked up from age 13-19. Too bad they didn't choose DeSoto. I have heard that it was one of the best in the state for rehabilitation, as the kids there wore khaki pants and golf shirts, the school was good, and you could learn a trade. There were guest cottages for visiting families and real psychologists provided therapy. I wish I had been placed there.

Because both my mother and father had lived or worked at the mental hospital and I was born there, I did a little research about it. For fifty years it was known as G. Pierce Woods State Mental Hospital, the largest employer in the little town of Arcadia, in central Florida. Nearly 1,000 people from the town and surrounding area provided care for the hospital's 285 mental patients. As a company town, Arcadia enjoyed a close relationship with the hospital, and the patients benefitted. The most improved patients could stroll, shop and dine in town, while townspeople enjoyed the hospital's 100-acre grounds and swimming pool for picnics. The people of Arcadia defended the hospital against accusations that its staff was poorly trained and it was unsafe.

I've never been to Arcadia, but it sounds real pretty. Live oak trees, white frame houses, a few antique shops and cafes, and other small stores selling cowboy boots and western wear. I wish I could have lived there—outside of the hospital, of course.

As my grandmother Lucille tells it, my mother, Sheila Boatman, was a top student and member of the swim team at John F. Kennedy Middle School in Clearwater until she suffered a head injury in a car crash. While in ninth grade, she was riding her bicycle home from school with her younger sister, my aunt Angie, when she was knocked off her bike, struck by a car driven by an older woman. She was hospitalized with head injuries and released.

"Everything changed from that moment on," my grandmother said.

"Sheila became addicted to drugs and alcohol, with wild mood swings and unpredictable behavior. She dropped out of school at age 15 and disappeared. I didn't hear from her for months. I filed a missing persons report, but nothing happened. Then one day I got a call from her from California. A strange man placed the call because he said Sheila came up to him and begged him to tell her where she was. Not what street, or what city, but where in the whole United States she was! She had no idea how she got to California. I bought a plane ticket for her to come home."

Hearing this as a young kid, I was amazed. How could my mother get across country to California at age 15? How could she not know where she was?

"What was wrong with her?" I asked my grandmother.

"She was diagnosed bi-polar, possibly psychotic, which is like being nuts," my grandmother said. "That was the first time she disappeared, but it happened again and again. She'd say she was going out for cigarettes, and I wouldn't see her for a year."

When my grandmother found out from the mental hospital that my mother was pregnant, she was furious. My Uncle Vic told me my grandmother got on the phone with someone from the hospital and yelled at them.

"Goddamit, I'm already raising one of her kids and I'm not going to raise another. You're the hospital, do something about it—abort the baby. We can't raise another one of her kids."

Vic said the hospital refused. Something about informed consent for an institutionalized mental patient. See, even before I was born people were arguing that they didn't want me.

"Hey, kid," Vic says when I remind him of my birth. "Grandma and I drove down to that mental hospital and brought you back here with us a few days after you were born. You didn't stay in the hospital very long, but your mother did, for a few more months."

"What did Grandma think of me?" I asked Vic.

"She took to you right away. You were a pretty cute baby," he said.

I love to read, especially westerns, mysteries and books about small towns. When I was in solitary confinement in the juvenile prison, I would rather read than eat, but they would never give me enough books. So I began to fantasize about my birth in a mental hospital. After all, how many people on this earth can say their mother got knocked up in a nuthouse, and then they were born there? When I don't get enough books, and I'm all alone, I imagine that it happened like this:

Old Doc Watson hangs up the phone in his office, wipes the sweat off his face with a pocket rag, grabs his black bag from the chair and hollers to his aging office nurse: "Lock up, Dolly. Looney Tunes is in labor. I'm gonna need your help as no one out there knows what they're doing when it comes to giving birth." As they drive the seven miles to the hospital, Doc reminds Dolly of the hospital's checkered past: "I know half the town works there,

Dolly, but they should have closed the place years ago. Hardly any shrinks on staff, patients screaming in the night, doped up on drugs, sleeping in the halls. Remember the patient who died of hyperthermia in a scalding hot bathtub?"

Doc and nurse scrub up inside a makeshift delivery room, surrounded by a few aides. They hover over a "mad" looking woman moaning in painful labor, holding her belly. "Don't even ask what drugs she has in her system," Doc whispers to Nurse Dolly. "Push, push, push," Doc urges Sheila, "push hard... harder...oh boy..." I pop out.

After I'm spanked on the butt and cleaned up, my mother Sheila gets to hold me and stroke my pink skin. She smiles at me. "There's my little boy, my Leo..." Now, I gotta tell you that Sheila did me a big favor then. I like the name Leo. Short and simple. Powerful. King of the jungle. Leo. (I found out later that my full name, Leo Lancing, was as close as my mother could get to Leah Lucille, the name of her older sister's eldest daughter.)

But Doc Watson has to spoil it by filling out the information form for the birth certificate. "Mother, Sheila Boatman. And who's the father?" No one answers, the staff looks uncomfortable, Sheila looks away. "Goddamit," Doc says, "how long has she been here?" "Close to a year," a nurse replies. "She won't tell us who. Maybe she doesn't even remember. She's been pretty heavily drugged. Could be another patient, could be a guard. Your guess is as good as mine."

Doc picks Leo up and cradles him, letting light from the window shine in his face. "Little Leo, you've got a grand name but a shitty start in life. God be with you."

I always feel better when I sink into that fantasy. I know the Doc cared. I'd thank him if I could find him. Do you know how many fucking times a kid gets asked in life who his father is? Do you know what it's like not to know one half of you, one half of your family, your relatives, your grandparents? Do you know when you talk to shrinks who think you're crazy,

you can't even help them out with a full mental health history? Do you think I should just say: "Name unknown, but a
wacko?" Or "name unknown, but a scumbag guard who raped
a doped up sick lady?" Or, do you think I should say, "They
didn't exchange names, just balled each other's brains out on
the night shift?"

Which would you choose?

Chapter 2

The Women I Loved

Sheila:

"Where are the children?" a woman's voice demanded.

"Show us the children," a man's deep voice followed.

"On what authority?" Dave asked, nearly yelling at them.

"Child protective services, under the sheriff's office. Consider us police."

My mother started to cry.

I opened the door to the closet and crept out towards the stairs. My mother's boyfriend Dave always told me to go in the closet when he and my mother argued or fought. But this time I heard the other voices, the voices of strangers, and my mother was crying. So I disobeyed Dave and stood on the top step, peering through the rails. I felt kind of brave for disobeying Dave. Then I was scared, because I saw the strangers downstairs with my mother and I heard the word "police."

There was a lady in a suit with the cops, and she was carrying a toy. I was almost four years old, and I hoped that the toy was for me.

In my earliest memories of Sheila, my mother, she is never alone. Whatever apartment she lived in, there was always a boyfriend with her. Before Rosie went to live with our grandmother, it was Bill. What I remember most about Bill is that he made my mother do all kinds of sexual acts in front of my sister and me. He took pictures of us naked. Bill said he was a deputy sheriff, but I doubt it. Sheila's next boyfriend was Dave, who would lock me in the bathroom as a punishment. I was always scared to be in a room by myself, so this drove me crazy.

Anyway, I must have made some noise by the banister that day because the lady started up the stairs and my mother started screaming.

"We're here under a court order to remove both kids," the lady said. "Please make it easier for them by getting them for us, together with some clothes, toys and snacks. They will be fine in our care, and you'll have a chance to talk to the judge tomorrow."

"Here's a notice of hearing, 8:30 tomorrow morning in Courtroom 14, the Criminal Justice Center in Clearwater." The man gave a paper to my mother. Dave ripped it from her hands.

"No, you can't take them...my babies...my babies."

Now I screamed. I heard Rosie crying somewhere else in the house and my mother kept screaming, "No, no, you can't take them..." pulling on the man's arm.

The lady in the suit climbed the stairs and took me by the hand, putting the stuffed animal in my other hand. I cried and tried to get to my mom, but the lady pulled me out the door to her car and drove off with me. I guess the man got Rosie. I learned later that he took her to my grandmother's house. She didn't want both of us that night. She had her hands full with my mother's antics and her own job. Rosie was easier to live with.

I always blamed Dave for this. I thought he made this happen to get rid of me so he could have my mother for himself. I didn't understand for a long time that the Department of Children and Families was involved. Later I learned that neighbors reported that I would play outside dressed in my underwear, no matter how cold it was, and that I was found playing in the street, in front of cars. Rosie was sent to look out for me, way too young. That's the last memory I have of living in my mother's house.

I've since read the report from the Department of Children and Families, written in 1990. It states:

"Mother appeared at the door with a T-shirt and a bikini bottom. She appeared disoriented and confused...Leo appeared initially nude and then put on his mother's coat. Leo appeared to be a healthy, attractive child...While there, the mother fed Leo a chocolate bar and chocolate milk for breakfast...About ten days later, another report was received for lack of supervision of Leo by mother, Sheila, in Tampa. Leo was picked up and taken into shelter.

"The mother often seems to be totally incapable of keeping up with these children. Today, she let Leo wander outside unattended away from home for 20 minutes...She once asked someone to help her locate Rose because the child had been missing overnight. When she was asked when Rose left home, she responded that she wasn't sure because she was away from home all night herself."

The lady in the suit took me to my very first foster home. I remember it was so crowded with so many kids that I had to sleep in a big cradle, even though I was almost four. I cried hard each day, and after about a week my grandmother came to get me. She told me it took her awhile because my mother's old boyfriend, Bill, tried to get custody of me, saying he was my real father. My grandmother showed the caseworkers photos of me in the nude that Bill had taken. She said that Bill was the one who called the cops and had me taken away. I never understood why I was taken away.

After that, I only lived with my mother when she and a boyfriend named Dave moved into my grandmother's house, and that was just for a little while. My grandmother didn't like Dave at all. For one reason, he got into a bad accident while Rosie and I were in his car. Dave and my mother were arguing with someone driving next to us in a big van. The van smashed into the side of us, destroying the car and throwing us into a ditch. Despite all this, I still loved my mother and wanted to live alone with her. My grandmother said that would never happen again. It really didn't matter because my mother and Dave left town.

It's weird how so many memories of my mother include sex. A few years later, while I was living with my grandmother, yet another guy named Dave and my mother moved into the garage in my grandmother's house. We called him "Dave, the pizza guy," because his job was delivering pizzas. When I was about eight, I remember swimming with my mother all alone in my grandmother's pool.

"Come here, Leo, my little man," she gestured to me. "Come closer. Mommy wants to look at her handsome guy. Come get on my raft, handsome Leo."

"Tell me the story again of how I got my name," I asked.

"Your cousin Leah, my sister Regina's girl, had the prettiest name. Leah Lucille. She's a few years older than you. I couldn't let that pass, so I named you Leo Lancing...Leo Lancing Boatman. That's as close as I could get and it's a beautiful name, don't you think so?

"Yes, I do."

Then she pulled me closer to her on the float and buried her head in my crotch. She pulled my bathing suit open and began to suck on me.

"My little man, my little Leo." For the three weeks that she and Dave stayed with us that time, she was always kissing my face, and when no one was there, sucking on my crotch. I denied it when asked because I was so embarrassed. But my mother had blabbed to her aunt about it, saying it "fulfilled my dream." My grandmother found out and ordered Dave the pizza guy and my mother to leave. My mother came back once with another dude she'd just met, but my grandmother was tired of her bringing men home, so she threw her out again. That's the last time I saw my mother.

I think about her often. She was a very pretty blonde, slim, about 5'7". I don't think anyone really understood her. She seemed dreamy, like she lived in a fantasy world. She always gave me a weird smile and would tell the craziest stories. She took a lot of pills. My grandmother said that she began taking pain pills after her bike accident in middle school and never stopped taking them.

When I was about 10, my mother was hitchhiking her way back to Florida from Colorado to visit us. She had married that guy Dave, the pizza man, but she was leaving him, going to divorce him. While hitchhiking, she got sick and passed out in a ditch along the road. Drunk and high on pills, she drowned in a small amount of water. A stranger found her, still holding a cardboard sign with the words "To Clearwater Florida" in big letters. She laid in the local morgue as a "Jane Doe" for a few months. Although my grandmother had filed another missing persons report, her address was now in New Port Richey, Florida, so the police didn't make the connection. Finally someone figured out that New Port Richey was the next town from Clearwater, and my grandmother was notified.

Although I hadn't seen her in a couple of years, I was upset and cried hard when I was told that my mother was dead. She was on her way back to see us and didn't make it. She had gotten rid of Dave the pizza guy. Maybe things would have been different. That thought made me very sad. She was the first woman I loved.

I'm told that I'm a good-looking guy and I do favor women. But when you've been locked up all your teenage years, and then again for life a few months later, there isn't much of a chance for romance. So, besides my mother, the other two women in my life who loved me are my sister, Rosie Boatman, and my grandmother, Ethel Lucille Boatman, who went by the name Lucille.

Rosie:

My older sister Rosie didn't look anything like my mother, but she too was always very pretty. Because Rosie's father was from Sri Lanka, she has kind of an exotic look, with long black hair. You could easily mistake her for Hispanic.

Rosie has always been a homebody: smart, caring, popular and observant. She always loved animals. She would raise money, do fundraisers, and sponsor a needy family at Thanksgiving. Rosie stuck up for me a lot, in fights with neighbor kids and even with my grandmother. She was the main person who made sure that I had at least one gift on birthdays and at Christmas.

But my grandmother always favored Rosie over me.

"I want my own ice skates. I want lessons like Rosie gets," I begged my grandmother again and again at an indoor ice-skating rink at the Countryside Mall in Clearwater.

"You be still and be quiet. If you're good and stop fussing, you can skate in the end when it's free skate." I was still mad, because free skate only lasted a few minutes, it seemed, but it was fun and I went as fast as I could, like hockey skating.

"Hey, speed skater. How'd you like to do a few chores around here?" It was the manager who took pity on me and made me his little helper, cleaning up and putting away the skates. I wore a little jacket like the people who worked there. He'd give me a couple of bucks, but I'd burn the money on video games instead of saving it to buy skates or lessons. I was only seven or eight years old, so not thinking far ahead.

"Rosie, you stink," I'd often whisper to myself watching her skate, but I didn't really resent her because she was a good skater, and I liked to watch her in all the fancy costumes my grandmother bought for her.

"Hi, Leo. Come with us." It was our neighbor, Pat, who took her boys skating. She noticed that my grandmother bought snacks and soft drinks for Rosie only, not for me. "Come with me and the boys, Leo. I'll let you pick out some treats." People can be kind when they spot an unfair situation.

Actually it was pretty easy to understand why my grandmother favored Rosie. She did what she was told. She didn't rebel or fight like I did. Her room was like a palace. She had a matching pink bedroom set, TV, a million Barbie dolls and dozens of other toys. My grandmother made skating dresses and doll houses for her. Later, she got her own dog and cat.

Maybe all girls are like this, but Rosie was *really* dramatic. She would exaggerate stuff that I did to get me in trouble, but then she was the one who would get between me and my grandmother when my grandmother was hitting me, screaming at me, chasing me around with a broom. Maybe she got me in trouble so that she could rescue me. I don't know.

"Leo took my doll...Leo ate all the Oreos...Leo punched me in the back...Leo hid my costume...don't yell at Leo...don't hit Leo...stop hitting Leo..." Rosie was like a broken record.

Lucille:

My grandmother Lucille was the strongest woman I've ever known and also the most difficult to get along with. She was a 5'2" bundle of energy, with curly short red hair. She walked so fast that I almost had to skip to keep up with her. Even when sick with cancer, she had a hell of a gait for a little woman. She grew up in Clearwater as part of an old Florida family, but moved to Springfield, Ohio, and then to Littleton, Colorado, before returning to Clearwater.

Now here's something interesting. Lucille had six children with six different fathers. Her oldest child, Grant, is almost 60 now, and her youngest, Vic, is 46. Grant owned a title company, became a millionaire and moved to South America. Gaylon, the next oldest, owns a drywall company in Florida. The two girls, Regina and Angela, married nice men and live comfortably. All of them have children doing well, and some have grandchildren. Sheila, my mother, is the only one who is deceased. The youngest, Victor, had some serious problems with the law but is now out of prison and trying to start over again in Colorado. He's tried to stay in touch with me, even when we were both in prison. He's half Panamanian as his father was a jazz musician from Panama. My grandmother met him on a cruise ship, where he entertained the guests. I guess by the time I was born my grandmother had had enough of men. I never saw a new man in her life.

My grandmother was often very sweet, well mannered, cultured and exactly what's expected of a Catholic woman who had raised many children and now two grandchildren. But she would fly into a sudden rage at times, shocking everyone, screaming, hitting, throwing things and breaking them. She spared Rosie but picked on me.

"Goddamit, Leo, you little shit. You got into my cookies again," she'd yell, chasing me around the house and yard and hitting me with sticks, brooms, whatever she could grab. Most of the time I deserved it, so I still loved her.

My grandmother worked in real estate off and on. She had so much extra energy that she opened a small restaurant in Clearwater called "Lucille's Kitchen." Rosie and I hung out there, eating grilled cheese sandwiches and talking to the customers, including an older guy named Leo who fascinated me. At some point we were evicted from my grandmother's home, so the restaurant became our home for a short time, until we got a rental.

Although I was only five and Rosie seven, we had a lot of freedom around the restaurant, playing in a big tree in the parking lot. I slept in the back of my grandmother's Bronco at night. In the morning before the sun rose, I would watch the sky slowly turn blue. I had no idea why I slept in the car when my grandmother and Rosie slept in the restaurant, but I wasn't afraid and actually it's a pretty nice memory I still have.

Grandmother Lucille always decorated the house up at Christmas, Easter and other holidays. She sang carols, made Easter baskets and sometimes took us to church. She got this idea that I would behave better if I made my First Communion, so she arranged that with a Catholic priest who chose a god-father for me. I don't think my behavior improved, but Greg, my godfather, became important in my life.

Because my grandmother had six children, I had a lot of cousins. I remember having a lot of fun when they came over to play. When I was about five or six, I went to live with my Aunt Regina and her boyfriend, Robert. I had mixed feelings about this because I had grown attached to my grandmother and I didn't want to leave Rosie. On the drive to their house they asked me to call them mom and dad, and they explained that my cousin, Leah, was now my sister. Robert was a mechanic, so I got to hang out at his shop a lot and "work" on the cars. Really, I just got in the way, but they let me. They were surprised that I couldn't write or spell my name, or even count past fourteen. They started to teach me right away and also bought lots of toys for Christmas and my birthday.

Uncle Vic told me that Robert really took to me. He didn't have any kids of his own. He told Vic he wanted to adopt me, before I had problems there.

"You really blew it," Vic told me much later. "That was a perfect placement for you and Robert was a great guy with a good job. You had it made, until you got out of control."

"It wasn't my fault," I told Vic. "I was so young, five or six. I didn't understand what to do now. I didn't know Robert wanted to adopt me. I wish he'd told me."

While I lived with Aunt Regina and Robert, my other cousins Tiffany, Crystal, Michelle, Kimberly, and Sharrie would come over to spend the night. Those are my Uncle Gaylon's five girls. One day in Robert's shop I tried to pick up and hug a dog. I didn't know that she was pregnant. She bit my face pretty bad. Another time my cousin Leah and I were tossing a metal airplane up and down and it hit me on the top of my head. I bled pretty badly, so much so that Aunt Regina rushed home from work and took me to the hospital to be stapled. She really did show me a lot of love.

One thing I didn't like there was that my room was on the other side of the house, far from the rest of the bedrooms. To find Aunt Regina, I had to go down a hallway, through a bathroom, through the kitchen and down another hallway. It was dark and scary, plus they had a lot of fruit rats, so I thought the house was haunted. I was only six. I started to get in trouble at school and got spanked when I got home. Nothing abusive, but one day I smashed all my toys and stuff. I was trying to figure out how they worked, what was inside them, and then I wanted to rebuild them myself. Man, that really got me in trouble.

One day I was trying to get something on a shelf and the whole shelf crashed down, smashing everything. Robert smacked me, not even that hard, but it left a big handprint across my face. The teachers saw it the next day. They tried to keep me out of trouble so I wouldn't get spanked at home, but one day a kid crawled under the table and put mustard on my new shoes. I wanted to get him in trouble, so I said I was going to get a spanking when I got home. The teacher called the state, and some dude came out to talk to me. I could tell by looking at Regina and Robert that I had really messed up. They asked me where I wanted to live, with them or Grandma? I was so ashamed. I was just six years old. I thought I was in trouble, so I blurted "Grandma" to get away. I immediately tried to take it back, but they wouldn't let me. I resented that a lot. You don't let a six-year-old make such a life-altering decision. So, it was back to Grandma. Still, I had a good two years with Regina and Robert.

When I was returned to Grandma right before my seventh birthday, I found things had changed. She wasn't as nice to me and now she clearly favored Rosie. She called me a "no good bastard" for "calling abuse on Regina after all she did for you." Rosie always had spending money. She got the biggest room of the house and also got to sleep on Grandma's bed. I was really starting to feel that I wasn't wanted.

The day I will never forget was all about a snow cone. I had a little change, and I heard the ice cream truck. I chased him down the street and bought a snow cone with all the money I had. When Rosie saw me coming back with only one snow cone, she threw a fit and locked herself in her room.

"Where's my cone?" she screamed. "Leo got a snow cone and I didn't."

"Shut up," I said.

I felt bad. I tried to give the snow cone to her or offered to share it, but she wouldn't open her bedroom door. Grandma heard us and she grabbed me and hit me, smashing the hard ice of the snow cone into my face until I was bleeding pretty good. I was used to her grabbing me by one arm and dragging me from one side of the room to another while hitting me with the other arm. But this time she was pounding my face with the snow cone, calling me a "greedy bastard" and—her favorite—"a no-good piece of shit." When she ran out of steam, she told me to get in the shower and wash off.

I was crying hard and when Rosie came in and saw all the blood on my face, she hugged me and washed me up. When I came out of the bathroom, Grandma had collected the pieces of the snow cone and put them in a cup. "You sit here and watch it melt you selfish, greedy little shit," she said to me. What was I supposed to do? I didn't get money or an allowance. It's all the change I had.

Rosie defended me a lot after that. "Stop hitting him, stop fighting with Leo," Rosie would yell at Grandma as she threw herself on top of me. It worked. Grandma would never hit Rosie.

Once Grandma caught both of us riding our bikes away from the house when we weren't supposed to. She chased us home with her car, almost running over us a few times, slamming the steering wheel and yelling at us. "Get back to the goddamn house, you brats." When we got home, she told Rosie to go to her room, and I got a whipping.

One of our babysitters saw the snow cone injuries and another neighbor saw me get a whipping after I took some money from Grandma's coin jar and bought a watch at the 7-11. The state was called both times, but nothing happened. We weren't removed. I just got in more trouble with Grandma. She said it was my fault "abuse was called." Things were bad now money-wise. We lived with one of Grandma's friends for a while, and then with Grandma's ex-husband Gilbert, a drunk who treated Grandma bad and was mean to me. He was only nice to Rosie, his doll.

A friend and I found some knives. I brought them to school and I was expelled. I couldn't be home alone, so Gilbert brought me to work with him. He had his own lawn cutting business. We stopped at one house where a really old man lived. The old man offered to get me some ice cream.

"Yes," I said. "I like ice cream. Almost any flavor."

"On your knees, kid," he said as he stood close to me. I dropped to my knees, thinking I was going to have to beg for the ice cream.

I watched as he stood over me, unzipping his fly. He pulled out his penis, touching my forehead with it.

"Suck this first, kid, and you'll get to suck on ice cream."

I had never done anything like that, but I did as I was told. He moaned and grunted and pulled his penis away as something wet dripped down my face.

Afterwards, I got sherbet. It wasn't even ice cream. I was disgusted but so embarrassed I didn't tell Gilbert or anyone.

A few weeks later Gilbert kicked us out of his house, keeping Grandma's furniture. The police said she couldn't get it back unless she had receipts.

These were bad times for Grandma. We stayed in a hotel a couple of nights until the money ran out. We ended up sleeping in her station wagon in parking lots, Rosie and I in the back and Grandma in the front seat. I was so proud of my grandma for seeing us through these hard times. It hurt to see her cry as she was trying so hard to raise us. She would drop us off at school and then go look for work and a cheap place to stay.

Aunt Gail, Grandma's youngest sister, took us in, but while we were there my cousin Anthony molested me and Rosie. The police made reports and we moved out and back to Gilbert's for a couple of weeks until Grandma rented a pretty nice house with a fenced backyard, dishwasher and swimming pool. That's where my mother visited us for the last time.

But bad things happened there too. My friend Chris and I were playing catch and I overthrew the ball. He ran to catch it and was hit and killed by a speeding car. I felt so guilty. Rosie's dog died, but she got another for her birthday. Rosie's birthday is 17 days before mine, and she's two years older than me. On her tenth birthday, Grandma had the house decorated with balloons and streamers. I blew up all the balloons. It was to be a pool party, but when all Rosie's friends came from her private school (yes, she still went to a private school), Rosie complained about my being there and Grandma ordered me to my room. That really hurt. Rosie had a big pile of presents on the table and I couldn't even watch her open them.

Seventeen days later it was my eighth birthday. No party and no friends. But we got to swim late into the night, and I did get a cake and a plastic bag of green soldiers from the Dollar General.

Either the birthday situation or my mother's last visit set something off with me. I trashed the house. My grandmother called the police. "I did it because I didn't get any money for my birthday," I told the policeman, but that wasn't true. It wasn't about the presents, it was the unfair amount of love that Rosie got, and how I was an afterthought. I didn't tell that to the police.

It's mixed up in my mind, because my mom's short stay with us then was so bizarre. "I'm going to buy you a woman, Leo, when I get some money. You need that," my mother told me. We hitchhiked everywhere and she gave me cigarettes to smoke. I was only eight, remember? She made me kiss her between her legs while on a float in the pool and then put my penis in her mouth. I was confused. A few days later when my mother asked me to suck her breasts, I refused. Shortly thereafter, she let a strange guy into our house.

"Grandma, Mommy brought a strange man here," I said. The two of them had a huge screaming fight, and my mother left. I never saw her again. I kind of felt if I had never said anything about the new guy, maybe my mother would still be alive.

I remember more hard times financially and moving around again, first to a friend of my mother's and then back to Aunt Gail, where Anthony lived and hurt me again. I learned not to say anything. Things were so tough for Grandma, for then she was diagnosed with breast cancer and the chemo treatments had her hair falling out. She still had lots of energy, but she blamed me for the stress that she said caused the cancer. Out of desperation, I guess, she put me on a plane to Illinois to stay in a home for orphans run by a Moose Lodge. I lasted just ten days, and they sent me back to Grandma. She said I'd messed up a good thing, but how could your real family send you to an orphanage? Maybe I didn't want to be home either, so I ran away with another kid. We got caught by the cops and returned home. When the police left, Grandma chased me with a hammer.

We were living in a duplex now. I had my own room, while Rosie and Grandma shared theirs. I was placed in a school for emotionally disturbed kids. I didn't last long there and was sent home where Grandma tried to home school me. That was a joke as all Rosie and I did was fight while Grandma was at work. She tried another group home, but I was sent back, and then my Uncle Vic got out of prison. That probably saved Grandma's life as Vic helped her take care of us. Sometime later he had to register as a sex offender.

My grandmother did formally adopt me, but then she gave me back to the state. I cried so hard when she put me in foster care again. I didn't understand it. After all, she kept Rosie. But as I look back, I see that I was a little hyperactive, maybe even wild, maybe a bit defiant.

My school grades were pretty good, but I was in trouble a lot. I was caught stealing cigarettes from the teachers' lounge. I didn't smoke them. My friend and I just filled my backpack with them until we were caught. We thought it was really funny that the teachers smoked so much. As punishment, I was suspended from school again. I was just too much for Grandma to handle, I guess.

My grandma visited me in the juvenile prison, however, and even brought Rosie with her twice. That's why I can never forgive the guards for what they did to me when my grandma passed away.

Chapter 3

The Men Who Loved Me

Vic:

"Hey, Rick," I said to one of my friends. "You've gotta meet my Uncle Vic. He's the cool uncle every kid wishes he had." He's about twenty years older than I am, but he acts like a kid.

"Vic's got a red-hot Alfa Romeo sports car and a tricked-out truck with all the gadgets."

It didn't take much for Rick and my other friends to like Vic. Who wouldn't like a cool ex-con who had a motorcycle, a boa constrictor, a dog named Peanut, pierced ears and plenty of drugs? His father was from Panama. He was an entertainer on a cruise that Grandma took one year. So, Vic had this half Panamanian kind of look.

When I was about five, he got married to Monica, who I thought was beautiful. I was the ring boy at their wedding, and my cousin Tiffany the flower girl, I think. The marriage didn't last too long. Looking back, I can see why. Vic was always just a big kid. But he wore good clothes, was in good shape, was smart and funny and in and out of prison a lot. My grandmother took Rosie and me to visit him in prison, which was real boring for me. He did teach me that you can make a living selling drugs, if you can handle prison life.

Just when Grandma couldn't take it anymore with me, when I was about eight, Vic was released again from prison. He started taking me to his mobile home for small periods of time, then longer. He bought me all new clothes. Life with Vic was one big party. He had a lot of young friends over and they'd come back from the clubs high and drunk. They smoked weed all the time. I was too young to mess with drugs. But I was also having problems in school.

"Leo, you're a smart kid," Vic said. "You get good grades, As and Bs most of the time. Think how well you could do if you didn't get kicked out of school so often? Genius level."

Apparently I was living with him when I was about nine years old, attending Seven Springs Elementary School in New Port Richey. Someone at the school called him to come get me.

"Leo, the place was a wreck. You were sitting in the classroom on the only upright chair, like you'd done nothing wrong. Nobody else was in sight. I asked you, 'Leo, what's wrong? What was that all about?'

"'I was mad at the teacher,' you said.

"The whole classroom had been evacuated. The kids were sitting outside on the lawn with their teacher. Inside the classroom, where you were, desks and tables and chairs were knocked over. The chalkboard was smashed to the ground. The place was a wreck. Why, Leo, why?

"You didn't answer, just grinned at me. That was the first of many calls to the school."

But Vic also told me that when not beating up kids, stealing their stuff or getting in trouble in school, I was lots of fun.

"You were very active. You loved camping overnight in tents, fishing, playing baseball and hockey games. You were a good hockey player; you loved the ice and the action."

What happened, Vic? Why did you make me leave?

Vic says the calls from the school got overwhelming, especially with his new job. I think it is because I stole forty dollars from him and got busted showing it all off at school. He wouldn't keep me anymore, which was probably a good thing.

Later on, when I was nineteen and let out of juvenile prison, I lived with Vic in his little tin can of a trailer. We were like brothers then. He wasn't in the best place in his life. He was bossy and was shooting coke. He was 41, and I thought he should get himself straight before telling me what to do all the time.

Anyway, about the time Uncle Vic sent me back to my grandmother's, she found another man to care for me.

Greg:

My godfather Greg was the best thing that ever happened to me. As I said, my grandmother was Catholic and she had this idea that since I hadn't even been baptized, a double dose of Baptism and First Communion might straighten me out. She took me to a Catholic church in New Port Richey to make the arrangements. The priest apparently agreed with her as he appointed a "godfather" for me. We went to Denny's Restaurant for our first meeting and Greg gave me twenty dollars.

A few days later I got sick at school and my grandma asked Greg to pick me up. I ended up staying with Greg for about three days. He used to be a nurse. Man, was I taken care of. I'd never had that much attention. I stayed in Greg's bed and watched TV, and Greg brought me sandwiches and all the juice I could drink. He took my temperature all the time and was very caring. He was an average size guy, about fifty years old. I don't think he had ever been married.

Soon, Greg started coming over to my house, taking me to the beach, the sponge docks and even up to New York and the Bronx Zoo. We stayed with a friend of his in New York City. It was the first time I'd gone out of state and my first time at a zoo. I loved watching all the animals at the zoo. I particularly remember the lion enclosure. Greg and I were on one of those sky rides overlooking the whole zoo. When we passed over the lions' den, one huge lion was standing on a big rock, trying to paw the car we were riding in. I leaned way out, and I swear I could have touched that lion's paw if we were going slower. "Get back here," Greg yelled, snapping my body back into the car. He was so freaked out. I thought it was funny.

I called Greg "Dad," and he seemed to like it. Mostly it was just the two of us. At his house, we'd wrestle a lot, watch movies or cook dinner. Greg was a perfectionist and a real nut on neatness. Everything had its place. "Wash your cereal bowl, Leo...pick up your clothes, Leo...put the game pieces back, Leo..." If you dirtied a dish, you would have to wash it right away. He was always worried about his water bill, so we took cold showers.

Greg seemed to be a real educated man. He didn't cuss much, just an occasional "damn." He didn't pick on me or belittle me. He even sent me to a summer day camp on a big lake in Tampa. I really liked the other kids and the huge playground.

I went back and forth between my grandma's house and Greg's home. On my ninth birthday, Greg bought me a really big kite. He also came for dinner that night when my grandma cooked a steak dinner with sliced tomatoes.

"I don't like tomatoes," I told Grandma.

"I cooked this special dinner just for you and by God you are going to eat the goddamn tomatoes."

Accidentally a tomato slipped off my plate. Grandma grabbed a steak knife and put it to my stomach. "I'll kill you, Leo," she yelled. She had been getting more violent, breaking dishes, throwing pans, hitting me with her high heels, clothes hangers and brooms. This time Greg was there, and he stopped her from hurting me.

Greg became a big part of my life. He took me fishing and hiking in Starkey Park. I actually taught him to fish, and he joked about that. He bought us both fishing rods and other equipment at a bait shop. We fished off the sponge docks in Tarpon Springs. If we caught any big fish, we brought them home to clean them and cook them for dinner.

Greg bought me toys and clothes. His parents were like my

grandparents. Greg took me to Daytona Beach where we rode the rides and walked on the boardwalk, munching on popcorn and other junk food. It was a great time and I felt truly loved. But, around this time my grandma was trying to get me adopted. Greg didn't want to adopt me, she said.

I went for a weekend to a family who was checking me out before adopting me. They had two sons already. They wouldn't let me ride their four wheelers. I chased them on their four wheelers until they called the police and wanted me gone. So much for that attempt.

Grandma was away out of state, so I was put in a group home and then a runaway shelter. It housed mostly girls, so I had the boy's room to myself until a 16-year-old boy was brought in and forced me to have sex with him. The counselors didn't believe me, but they let me sleep on the couch until Grandma picked me up again.

When Grandma brought me home, I got in fights with her and Rosie, and Grandma whipped my ass again. Then, when I ate almost a whole package of Oreo cookies, Grandma hit me so hard with a broom that she knocked loose a couple of my teeth. I ran away, this time to Greg's house and the state began a background check on him to see if I could live with him. Something short of adoption. In the meantime, I stayed at Jody Patterson's foster home. She had a farm with horses, and it was a fun 21 days until Greg was approved.

I went happily to Greg's house. We did something fun every weekend, like vacations in Daytona, the beach, fishing and so on. He took me to the sponge docks in the Greek town of Tarpon Springs and taught me about harvesting sponges and watching the divers off the boats. We toured some of the larger boats docked in Tarpon Springs. Greg was always teaching me something about how people make a living. He sometimes took me to work with him. He was a neat guy and always wore a short-sleeved buttoned up shirt and khaki shorts right above his knees. My behavior in school at this time was perfect. I think it was the best time of my life.

During the short time I actually lived with Greg, I learned to love the outdoors. I have a special memory which I bring to the surface during dark moments or days. It's the two of us, Greg and me, hiking in Starkey Park in nearby Pasco County.

"Hey, Leo," Greg would say. "Not so fast. You've heard of 'stop and smell the roses?' Well, I want you to stop and look at these different trees. The park rangers have made it easy for you. They have identifying signs next to them. You walked right by some."

I traced my steps backwards. I saw the white signs: Slash pine, live oak, scrub. "I got it, Greg. You can tell me about the trees at home. I want to catch sight of some animals."

We'd spend all day on the park trails, sometimes going exploring off the trails. "Here's an armadillo, or a tortoise," Greg would say. "Watch out for the snakes. Don't startle the raccoons."

"Greg, help me with this walking stick," I'd say, handing my clumsily half-carved stick to Greg to finish. He was an amazing wood carver, fast and artistic.

"These sticks aren't just for walking, Leo. Use them to knock the spider webs out of the way on the trails. You don't want to mess with any nasty spiders on these trails."

The park featured a few log cabins that you could rent for camping. I remember the first time we camped for a weekend. I was setting up my bunk when I heard Greg shout.

"Don't move, Leo."

I heard the sound of Greg's stick swishing through the air above my head. I looked up in time to see a huge black spider scurrying towards the rafters.

The cabins all shared one bathroom, I mean shared it with spiders, snakes and about 20 armadillos. They scatter like Hell when you opened the door but would return seconds after you left. I guess it was more their bathroom than ours.

Greg knew how to teach me chores in a fun way. "You can use the stuff I'm going to teach you all your life, Leo. Chop some more wood, build us a fire. I can even teach you survival skills when you get older."

I was dog tired the first night, so surprised when Greg woke me up in the dark.

"Come on, kid," he said. "The sun's about to rise and you're going to miss a beautiful sight unless you get out of that bunk and follow me."

Our cabin was the last in the row, next to a large field with chest-high grass. We crept onto the edge of the grass, and right in front of us were four or five nice size does. I'd never seen deer up close. In fact I'd never camped before, or explored trails in the woods.

Like any nine-year-old, I couldn't sit still and watch them. I got up to chase them, and when I got about eight feet nearer to them, they took off, me running through the tall grass after them, arms flailing, and Greg laughing his head off.

It was a blast, but it's just a wonderful memory now.

Then a few nights later, at Greg's home, he asked me to come upstairs to bed with him and I said I wanted to stay downstairs and watch a movie on TV. The next morning, a lady from the state showed up to get me, and Greg had packed all my clothes and stuff. Maybe Greg just wasn't ready to raise a kid. Or maybe he wanted to become a priest, like he told me sometimes. I only saw him one more time, when I was in foster care. Not a good memory. I missed him a lot.

After Greg's, I was taken to another foster lady's house whose husband was dying of cancer.

"Grandma, please, please come and get me. It's too sad here," I begged to her on the phone. That's when she told me that she signed away her rights to me and that I could send her to jail. I was only nine. I was speechless. Shortly after that I was Baker Acted to a mental health hospital, The Harbor, for threatening my foster mom. They shot me full of drugs to control my behavior. The needles in my butt hurt and left bruises. There were kids there much worse than me. I saw people cutting themselves, smashing their faces against a wall, passing out in group therapy and drooling all over the floor. I was in and out of two more foster homes and back to The Harbor for at least a month because I aimed a bow and arrow at my newest foster parents.

I never saw my grandma during this time, and I never lived with her again. I didn't see Greg either, although he wrote to me. I thought about Greg every day. I still do. Looking back, I think my time with Greg was the greatest missed opportunity of my life so far. We had so many good times together. If I'd just gone upstairs to bed with him, who knows how my life would have turned out?

Archie:

Archie was the next man who loved me, who tried to take care of me, who still writes to me in prison and sends a little money for the canteen. What can I say about Archie? I know I'm not going to throw him under the bus like others want.

"I forgive you Archie," I whisper to myself, thinking he might hear it somehow.

I first met Archie in The Harbors, a psychiatric hospital. The court appointed him to be my guardian when my grandma gave me back to the state. He was older than Greg, short, with old-fashioned clear glasses. He'd never been married or had a family. He was what you would call "socially awkward," a little weird, but he really wanted to adopt me.

He took me home from the hospital and the different foster homes for weekend visits. We went boating and fishing. He had to get the paperwork completed to adopt, but he didn't get a chance as I kept running away from him and from the foster homes.

I called Archie "Dad," and although I've forgiven him, I won't forget that he too used me for his pleasure. Sex was frequent, sometimes painful, sometimes not. I think he truly did love me and still does. He is the one person that visited me more than once or twice in juvenile facilities and sometimes in prison. As I said, he sends letters, writing supplies and sometimes a little money for the canteen. That's a lot for him because he lives very frugally.

I've been told that Archie still keeps a sexy picture of me when I was about twelve on his computer screensaver. I'm shirtless, in jeans and my white briefs are showing. Maybe like a Calvin Klein ad, or so I've been told.

I know that Archie still cares for me. I don't want to lose that relationship. I just wish I hadn't run away so often. Perhaps then, Archie could have adopted me and none of the awful things that happened later would have taken place. Or if they had just rushed through the adoption, I wouldn't have run away. Which is it? Who knows? Who cares now? I just know that Archie is the one person who has kept in touch with me, even now, and I don't want to drive that person away.

Archie writes to me in prison, and I write back to him right away. Here's a letter from me to him:

"Dad,
It was very good to hear from you. Mail call came and I had three envelopes, all from you. Paper, envelopes, post cards sent to me at Charlotte jail and of course your letter. It made me feel real good and cared about. It's awesome to have you out there and in my corner... Keep me updated on your search for a boat as well as any projects you got going on. Listen, I know my thought process may not always be right, and I know I'm not the best person in the world, but I do feel and I do care. I appreciate everything you have done for me, and I do love you. I hope you know and feel that. I wish that I could explain myself better sometimes. But thanks for being there. Leo"

Authors Note: ACEs is a term used by psychologists and therapists to evaluate the effect of childhood trauma on their adult patients by using a 10-question test of adverse childhood experiences. (ACEs). Evidence shows that the toxic stress of trauma to a child, especially when pro-longed, can interrupt normal physical and mental development and cause lifelong issues. Most people score very low on the test; Leo would have scored a perfect 10.

Chapter 4

Foster Care
1996-1999

I was ten years old when I was discharged from yet another crisis admission to a mental health facility. I went from there directly to the foster home of the meanest man I'd ever met.

I'd been Baker Acted for a few days for suicidal thoughts and misbehaviors and somehow the state thought this foster dad would straighten me out. This placement happened after numerous child abuse investigations of my grandmother, who continued to yell, scream, hit and throw things at me when I lived with her. Then she gave me back to the state. She canceled her adoption of me.

My Uncle Vic told me that when my grandmother called the state to tell them they were now in charge of me, she screamed into the phone, "I told you to abort him. I told you not to let him be born. I told you I couldn't raise another of her children. But you went ahead anyway, so now he's all yours. You take him."

I repeat: I was only ten years old. If you've read the first three chapters of this book, you know I'd been through a lot in those ten years. But for the next three years I was physically and mentally tortured by a sicko who got off abusing foster kids. His name was Tony Bryant. I spent some weekends visiting my grandmother, Greg, and later Archie when I lived with Tony, but I was always returned to Tony. That was my official placement, my official punishment.

Tony and his wife Pam were "therapeutic" foster parents

under Suncoast Mental Health services. "Therapeutic" meant that they were paid more than regular foster parents for taking care of troubled kids and that one of them had to be home with us. Only one could work outside the home. Tony's wife, Pam, worked as a teacher. Tony ruled the roost at home. Pam did the cooking, though, and she sure did know how to cook. That was the only good thing about the placement. The food was good.

Tony was a short Black man in his early 50s. He was heavy, but also muscular and very athletic. His upper body was barrel-shaped, but his legs were muscular and in great shape. He played doubles tennis almost every day at Northwest Park, so he kept in shape. He normally dressed in a T-shirt, gym shorts and tennis shoes. He gambled at the dog track many nights.

In their home, six of us were piled into a small bedroom with two bunk beds and a folding bed in the middle of the room. Queen, Calvin, Kenny, Steve, Billy and I lived in that room for the most part of three years. When Archie would pick me up from Tony's home for a night or weekend with him, he liked to hear me describe them:

"Queen, seven, was a mentally challenged kid the Bryants had adopted. He was blonde and really good looking. The type that all the moms go gaga over. He had the mind of a four-year-old. I liked him and I tried to be patient with him. The other boys often hit him out of frustration and then Queen would get us all in trouble.

"Calvin, a six-foot tall young adult, was also mentally challenged. He had an awkward body and huge hands that were always bent at the wrist unless he was using them. Calvin was put in charge of us when Tony and Pam were both gone. He tried to have sex with Queen and Kenny.

"Billy was about eight years old, a quiet kid with

brown hair. I don't remember much about him as he left shortly after I arrived.

"Kenny was my size, black-haired, with a limp. He was the tagalong. We always said, 'Let's show Kenny how to be cool.' He was kind of a weakling, but he was always pushing buttons until Steve or I snapped. When I last saw Kenny at the Pasco Juvenile Detention Center, it was like 'Holy Shit!' He was huge, about 6'4" and well built. I thought that no one could whip him now, but man, he was still the lame old Kenny and very timid. He had a hard time fitting in with the other kids.

"Steve was three years older than me, about thirteen, Black like the foster dad, Tony. He was still in fifth grade, in class with me. He was the only one who Tony bought brand new clothes for and went easier on the punishment, so naturally I wondered if it was because they were both Black. Maybe it was because Steve was built like a body builder, freakishly, for his age.

Bruce Michaels, called Mike, was our case manager. I really liked Mike. We all looked forward to his visits. He made us laugh and was easy to talk to. But when we complained about Tony, he didn't believe us.

"Mike," I'd say, "who can do 1,000 jumping jacks? It's impossible. Tony sits in his chair drinking beer and watching us. When we fall on the floor because we're so tired from the jumping jacks he picks us up and throws us against the wall." I showed Mike the blisters on my feet.

"Leo, kid, you ran away barefoot a few days ago. You probably got those blisters then," Mike told me.

Darn right I ran away barefoot, and when the police brought me back, Tony made us strip naked and run through the house. He thought if we were naked, we wouldn't run away. He was right. We even faked suicide attempts. At least then we were taken to a hospital and shot up with drugs for a few days. It was better than Tony's home.

"Please get us out of here," we'd beg Mike, often in tears. But he still didn't believe us. Maybe he didn't want to be the whistle-blower? Maybe he fell for Tony's reputation for being tough on troubled kids? But how could he not know how bad it was?

I became an angel at school, making the honor roll and getting straight As sometimes. School was a way to get away from Tony, and I loved being there. I even had a favorite teacher, Mrs. Whales, at Northwest Elementary School. My favorite subjects were science and history. It was a complete turnaround. I would do *anything* to stay in school. Before that, I was always in trouble in school, running away, uncontrollable, failing classes.

When I was eight, I had been expelled from school when another kid and I found some cool knives in an abandoned house near the bus stop and made the mistake of taking them to school to show them off. That's the kind of stuff I pulled. But at Tony's I learned to behave at school just to keep away from Tony. Can you believe that was used against me?

"Hey, kid," Mike would say when I complained. "You're doing great at school. It can't be so bad here with Tony or your teachers would be calling us. They'd see the bruises from the beatings. They haven't done that."

"Frog walk, Mike," Billy complained. "You know what it's like to walk around the house naked, walking like a frog? Get us out of here, please, Mike."

Many times when we got home from school, Calvin would be the only one at home. He was supposed to watch us for an hour or so until Tony showed up. One day when we were alone with Calvin, Kenny wanted something from me.

"I want your Scarface cassette tape," he said. "The one with the curse words, before Tony gets home."

"Tony took it from me," I told him. "It's in his back room.

I think in the dresser in the back."

"Okay. If you keep an eye on Calvin, I'll sneak back and get it."

I figured, what the hell? If Kenny's going to break the rules, what's the risk to me? So while I watched Calvin, who was watching TV, Kenny snuck into Tony's back room. Soon, he returned all excited about something and dragged me into our bedroom. He showed me three $100 bills.

"Holy shit! Are you crazy?"

"Man, this is just part of his stash. He probably won't even miss it until way down the road," Kenny said.

Well, to be honest I hated Tony and living there was pure hell. I was always running away. I got to thinking that three hundred dollars would help us get pretty far away, so I convinced Kenny that the only way I would be part of his theft was if he agreed to run away with me.

You would think we would just hit the door with the cash, but it wasn't that easy. The front door was padlocked. Calvin kept the keys around his wrist on a little rubber bracelet. All the windows were nailed or screwed shut.

"Take this spoon," I told Kenny. "Let's try to work a nail loose from this window."

Calvin was already suspicious as he saw Kenny come from Tony's back room, acting like he was using the hallway bathroom, so he snuck in on us as we were trying to loosen the nail.

"Don't tell on us," Kenny pleaded with Calvin, but Calvin called Tony, who was right down the street.

We tried to kick the window open, but Tony got there before we could get out.

"I think they were in your bedroom," Calvin told Tony.

I knew we were already in trouble for trying to run away, so I said, "Kenny was just looking to try to get the back door open."

Well, I don't know how, it's like Tony was able to read minds, because he ran to his dresser to check on the money and came back in a complete rage. He grabbed Kenny and me by our necks, slamming us into the wall repeatedly and threatening to kill us if we didn't tell him where the money was.

"Here it is, all of it," Kenny said, taking the crumpled bills from his jeans pocket.

"If either of you ever steal from me again, nothing in the world will keep me or my family from running you down and killing you."

Then, he made us exercise. Jumping jacks, sit-ups, running in place. We had to do it all through the night in the hallway while he watched from his rocking chair, watching TV. Anytime we slowed down he'd yell, slap us around or slam us into the floor. By the time we were done, our feet were swollen, we had black and blue marks all over us, and we hadn't any food or water.

"Okay, you can stop now and go sit at those desks," Tony told us at about 3 a.m. The desks were in separate corners of the living room. He wouldn't let us go to bed or to the restroom. He took our clothes away and gave us towels to cover up. We had to sit at those desks for two days, except for meals and bathroom breaks.

When Tony decided we were ready to return to school, he walked with us so we wouldn't run away.

"Let's go for it," I yelled to Kenny and took off running, but Kenny chickened out.

Tony ran after me, but I had a good head start, plus I was scared shitless of what would happen to me if I got caught. I cut through a big field right next to Northwest Elementary School, and as I was running, I saw Tony's van coming at me. It was like something out of a movie scene. He literally hopped the curb and came at me.

"Get in the van," he yelled at me.

No way, I thought. I cut through the neighborhood behind the school so he couldn't chase me. I was called in as a runaway and picked up by the police. Amazingly, Tony didn't hit me when I returned. Probably because the police were there.

Not only did Tony nail our windows shut and padlock the door so we wouldn't escape, he put a baby monitor in the room so he could catch us if we talked to each other. In the hallway he put a rocking chair with an alarm on it that would go off if we tried to leave the room. All the doors in the house were kept locked or stuck shut. The bathroom didn't work, and we were never allowed outside to play with other kids. It was like a prison. Our crime was that we were foster kids.

Tony left us alone with Calvin a lot so he could place bets at the dog track or play tennis at Northwest Park. When home, Tony ruled with an iron hand. He used outrageous punishments in order to keep us in line. I once overslept and missed my school bus. For that he yelled at me, slammed me around and made me do 1,000 jumping jacks. No, I could never finish 1,000 jumping jacks and neither could anyone else. We were made to leap around like frogs. If we got into a fight, he would take the winner out back to fight him. He'd make us sit naked on a towel to keep us from running away.

Tony enjoyed humiliating us in public. One time we were supposed to be watching Queen at the park while Tony played tennis, and Queen wandered off. Tony made us stand in the corner of the tennis courts and do 1,000 jumping jacks while people were playing tennis. Maybe I should have watched Queen more closely, but I was only ten.

Tony confiscated whatever gifts or clothes people gave us. Archie, my guardian, bought me a backpack and Tony took it. He never bought us new clothes but took everything from us and put it in a back room, saying it was for "safekeeping." We never saw those things again. He gave away whatever clothes came into his house to those he thought needed it, mostly his family.

On my eleventh birthday my godfather Greg took me to the mall and bought me a Walkman and tapes. I'd never had anything like that before. I was so happy to be with Greg, and I loved that new Walkman. As soon as Greg brought me back to the foster home, Tony took the Walkman and tapes from me.

"Give me those things," Tony said. "The boys are going to break them." I never saw that Walkman again. That was also the last time I saw Greg, although he wrote to me a couple of times.

Christmas holidays at Tony's foster home were the worst. We were normally in some kind of trouble, Tony's "doghouse," as he called it. Tony would retaliate against all of us if one of us did something he didn't like. He would line us up in a row and scream at us until someone confessed. Then he would punish all of us. He would sit in his chair drinking beer and watching TV, forcing us to do 1,000 jumping jacks. Then we were made to watch other people in his family open Christmas presents. Sometimes on school days, he would keep us home and make us sit all day and sleep on a desk facing the wall. Punishment for running away.

It hurt me even when other kids got in trouble. Calvin smacked Queen one day. Tony yelled that he was going to take Calvin outside and "beat his ass." He did just that, and we could all hear Calvin screaming and crying.

Now I have to admit that sometimes Calvin or one of us would make up something terrible to see if Mike would take us seriously. Once someone said that Tony tried to have sex with Queen while his wife, Pam, was away, and that when she came back and found out, he beat her up so bad that she was taken to the hospital. That was investigated by a bunch of people, but it turned out not to be true, and the reason Pam was in the hospital was that she was sick with pneumonia.

Steve, Kenny and I began running away and then committing crimes. We knew that if we got caught, we would be taken to the juvenile detention center for a while. Although locked behind bars in prison suits wasn't fun, it was a lot better than being with Tony. We learned that if we committed certain serious crimes, like arson, we'd have to spend twenty-one days in the detention center. So guess what? We started set-ting fires when we ran away. First, we'd shoplift a couple of cigarette lighters from a convenience store. Then, we would gather old cardboard boxes, broken down for the garbage col-lectors in back of a grocery store. Then, we would pick our target. After a few tries we set fire to a hot dog stand and got caught. That's just what we wanted. Twenty-one days in the detention center.

Some kids cry and beg to get out of detention. Not us. The food in detention was pretty good. We went to school on-site each day. After that, we had a big fenced-in area for basketball and football. We played kickball a lot and watched movies. There were other kids to talk to and play with. The guards treated us pretty well. Compared to Tony's home, it was heaven.

Did we tell our case workers about Tony's abuse? Yes, but they didn't believe us. Mike told us not to "press the issue." At that time Tony was known as a great guy who turned problem kids around. I guess he did for a while because foster kids were so scared of him. Mike also told Tony about our allegations, I guess as part of an investigation. Then Tony really retaliated. He padlocked our door to keep us inside our room. He'd set an alarm to see if we used the bathroom. No wonder we began to run away.

A few years later, when I was sixteen and locked up in Omega, a juvenile prison, state officials interviewed me about abuse in the Bryant home. They interviewed Steve, Billy and other foster kids. They filed a report that confirmed every-thing we'd told them: the jumping jacks, the beatings with belts, Calvin's sexual aggression while he watched pornogra-phy and begged for oral sex, and Tony's drinking. Here's the summary of the investigator's findings from a report that I was given to read:

> "It should be noted that the four children in the home,
> as well as five children who lived as foster children

in the home at varying times in the past, were inter-viewed. There was no question that there was a pattern of abuse which spanned over at least seven years. The current foster children were removed from the home, as was their adopted son."

Three simple phrases. "No question." "Pattern of abuse." "Spanned over at least seven years." That was my life for three years beginning when I was ten.

I also read Department of Children and Families records from when I was eleven and twelve and state workers inter-viewed me and the other boys at Tony's home. We told them about the frog exercises, the jumping jacks, why we ran away, the beatings and sexual stuff.

Here's what they wrote about our allegations: "All of the residents at the foster home are made to do 1000 exercises as punishment. If they do not complete the exercises the fos-ter parent (Tony) picks them up and throws them across the room. Leo and another youth ran away from the foster home recently and were taken to the juvenile assessment center. Leo has bruises on his back from being thrown and blisters on his feet from the exercises. If any resident at the foster home runs away and has to return, Tony gives them 10 seconds to strip naked and run through the house. Both Leo and another youth have attempted to kill themselves with the hope that the attempt would take them out of the foster home."

Despite this report and complaints from all the foster boys, the state found "no indicators of abuse" and that the Bryants are "very good foster parents." The state labeled us "emotionally disturbed." It took them five years to find out that we were telling the truth.

While in prison, I read earlier records of a foster child in Tony's home complaining that he was beaten with an exten-sion cord and pipes, then changing his story, probably because he was afraid of Tony. My lawyers told me later that Tony lost his foster care license. I hope he never gets it back.

So how did I feel years later when we were vindicated and the state admitted that all the abuse indeed had occurred? Did I feel hurt, crushed, or angry that none of our caseworkers believed us about Tony? Did I feel triumphant years later that the state finally believed us and shut down Tony? Actually, none of those. Looking back, I think I mainly felt frustrated that they didn't seem to care. I got used to feeling frustrated. I almost expected it. At Tony's foster home I came to believe that no one would help me. I had to help myself. I did it by running away and breaking the law.

Chapter 5

Delinquent Acts
1999-2001

"You're charged with four counts of burglary, four counts of criminal mischief, three counts of larceny, carrying a concealed weapon and vehicle theft," the judge in his black robe sitting high on his bench read to me in court. "And you're only twelve years old."

In the three months before January 19, 1999, I committed those crimes with Kenny, mostly to get out of Tony's home and into the juvenile detention center if we weren't successful at running away. Kenny and I started a fire in the shrubbery behind the Dogwater Café, a glorified hot dog stand. This time Kenny was as eager to get out of Tony's house as I was.

We vandalized a public utility office and stole equipment which we found there. We broke into Northside Christian School. I took money from my grandmother's purse while spending the night visiting her. I was in and out of the juvenile detention center, which was a whole lot better than Tony Bryant's house. When I was returned to him, I would run away again. Then I stole an automobile, and I was caught with a concealed weapon.

Those crimes were enough to get me sentenced to San Antonio Boys Village, a Level Six, moderate-risk juvenile commitment program. It was located in San Antonio, Florida, in the middle of the state, home of the annual rattlesnake festival. You may think it was about time, given the number of crimes I'd committed. However, what's unusual in my case is that I was never placed on probation. I never got the chance to improve my behavior with the help of a well-trained, compassionate juvenile probation officer. I never received juvenile delinquency services in the community. The judge sent me straight to a lockdown program, probably because he thought I was out of control due to my age and the number of crimes I'd committed.

Given that I was only twelve years old, and that the crime spree occurred while I was living with Tony Bryant, I think a juvenile probation officer on my side, together with another foster placement, could have straightened me out. Maybe then I wouldn't have run away so much. Maybe Archie would have been able to adopt me. Maybe everything after that happened to me and to those people I murdered wouldn't have occurred. It's a huge "maybe," but I think about it all the time.

I was supposed to be in San Antonio for six to nine months. I left the place three times: once to be taken to The Harbors for mental health treatment because I was out of control and twice when I escaped.

I told the people at The Harbors that I had "impulse control disorder," because someone told me that. But I was returned to the Boys Village within a few days. Looking back now, San Antonio was actually a good program with tons of activities. I probably should have settled down and stayed there. But I didn't like being locked up for so long. I thought it was unfair. The man in charge, Mr. Messic, a nice guy, told me:

"You're very smart, Leo, but very hyperactive. You need to be kept very busy and you need to stay out of fights. You're the youngest and smallest kid here, barely thirteen when you were admitted. You're not even five feet tall. You weigh less than 100 pounds. You're no match for the bigger guys, so don't pick fights. Keep your nose clean. Study hard. You'll do fine here if you obey the rules."

I wish I'd listened. Indeed, I was an easy target because of my small size, but I was a fighter too. Even kids who were my friends became my enemies. And I was always trying to run away.

My escapes didn't last long. The first time I was barefoot and shirtless, and also handcuffed. So even though they couldn't catch me, I didn't feel like wandering around in the country like that, so I turned myself in. The second time, Kareme Mitchell and I ran, but the dogs caught us in a cow field about three miles away, so that was that. We surrendered without any resistance. After about six months at San Antonio, they decided to transfer me to a more secure facility. Had I known what was in store for me, I probably wouldn't have escaped from San Antonio.

"We can't deal with you here, Leo," Mr. Messic said. "You're being transferred to Sago Palm Academy, a level eight, high-risk, juvenile residential facility in Pahokee, Florida. Good luck there."

Sago Palm Academy:

This happened in the spring of 2000, three months before my fourteenth birthday. I was still only 4'11" tall and I weighed just 98 pounds. Sago Palm was a *very, very* violent world. I mean this was just like real prison. Gangs controlled everything and fighting was an everyday thing. More than 180 boys were housed there, all running around doing whatever they wanted. The cellblocks housed 32 inmates in two-man cells. Rarely was a fight one-on-one because the gangs jumped in. The place was out of control, so I became just as wild. I joined a gang for protection and because it was cool. We would fight a lot, and I mean a lot!

The staff regularly encouraged us to fight. If you went to

them about a problem, they might tell everyone else you were a snitch. I think the staff encouraged the gangs to control each other by fighting. In the beginning I rose in rank to a position of authority, but I was still one of the youngest and the smallest there, and the other boys didn't like taking orders from a little white boy, so they beat me bad. My entire body was covered with bruises. I reported the abuse, and the investigators took pictures of me.

I had dozens of cell mates, all kids like me. The food was like school food in a regular public school, small trays. I didn't do much recreation. Because I was always the youngest and smallest, I wasn't picked very often for the football and basketball teams. Kids who got some money from family bought marijuana from some of the guards. Sometimes they gave it to me. The guards didn't mind. They thought it made us more passive.

Although it was called an "academy," Sago Palm was more like a prison. It was so different from the San Antonio Boys Village. One of my cell mates sexually molested me and it wasn't reported to staff until a week later. A guard named Miller targeted me. He hated me. He got one of the lady counselors to lie and press charges against me. Originally, all I got was a disciplinary referral for tapping her on the shoulder to get her attention. When Miller heard about it, he told her to say I punched her. That turned into a felony battery on my record, but I thought if I pled to it, admitting it, even though I didn't do it, I would be transferred out of there. That turned out to be a huge mistake.

I picked up charges right and left, thinking I'd be transferred out of Sago Palm. I climbed on top of a basketball goal and later a tree to get away from the abuse. I used ink to make tattoos on my arms, to make me appear tough. It took nine months before I got any mental health treatment or therapy, supposedly for grief and loss. I'm not sure it did any good at all, because I was charged with hitting a teacher, swallowing medication I'd stolen from the medical office, and striking another teacher, this time a pregnant one, after exposing myself to her.

The one cool guy at Sago Palm was Mr. Moreland, one of my unit managers. He knew how to talk to us and to try to keep order. Each cell block, one of which housed all the sex offenders and perverts, had four units with a unit manager, a sergeant and two guards. I wanted to be kept busy. I tried. But how do you keep busy when you're always locked up?

Up until this time, the residential programs I was locked up in were called detention centers, or villages or academies, not actual prisons. They are supposed to be rehabilitative, not punitive like prisons are.

Well, all the charges I racked up got me what I thought I wanted—out of Sago Palm. Just before my fifteenth birthday I was transferred to a level ten maximum-risk facility near Sarasota run by the Manatee County sheriff's office. I guess they gave up on trying to rehabilitate kids there because the name of the new place was Omega Juvenile Prison.

$$Chapter\ 6$$

2001-2005

Omega Juvenile Prison was a military-style boot camp that turned into a combat zone. But this time the kids weren't fighting each other; the guards were fighting the kids.

The overall concept was actually pretty good. The problems come with inexperienced guards who don't understand military bearing and discipline. When I first got there, most guards were ex-military. It was strict, hard but fair. Then they were replaced with other guards who were ignorant and thought that the way to be strict was to use personal information to taunt and goad you. The psych unit often gave our mental health history or abuse history to the guards, who would laugh about it and use it against us. A guard teased me when my grandmother died. He said she'd given me away, never loved me. For no reason other than to get me to go off. That's sick.

There were some good guards. I remember Deputy Swells because he was kind to me and talked to me.

"Hey, Leo. How's it going? You had a good day today. Keep it up. Maybe I can get you some more books to read."

Deputy Kauffman, on the other hand, seemed to enjoy being mean. He'd slam me smack in the head, one time chipping my teeth. He'd hold his fingers like an imaginary gun to his head, saying, "If I had my choice..." Talking was forbidden. Some guards would beat the crap out of you for just talking or asking a question. During the first years I was there I was written up for minor things, like failing to raise my hand in class or moving my eyes while in detention. The rules made it way too hard.

One year we got a new inmate, Derrick King, from Pensacola, one of the two brothers who murdered his father. That's the kind of kid who needed a juvenile prison. Not me. I got worse, not better, in Omega.

When I was still fifteen, I spent two months in solitary confinement. Nothing but food and water pushed through the door for two months. It was so horrible that I can't talk about it.

Omega is the type of facility that systematically de-humanizes people. The more cruel you are to a person, the harder their heart becomes and the more hate they develop for their fellow man. They hide the pain and hurt created by becoming emotionless and mean-spirited. This way what you do to them won't hurt them. I arrived at Omega just before I turned fifteen and left just after my nineteenth birthday. I lived through more than four straight years of this brutal treatment.

The education I received at Omega was the only good thing about the place. Although classes were often canceled, I got my high school diploma. They encouraged me to take the GED test instead, but I refused and made them give me a regular diploma. I'd earned it. I'd passed the tenth grade FCAT test and even got a letter from the governor. I wanted to take some college courses online, but they said they needed me to fill the high school slots, so I waited to get my regular diploma. The classes were the only thing that made me feel like a normal kid, a student.

Holidays were the worst because the teachers were on vacation, so you spent all day in your cell. We had a basket-ball court but were never allowed to play, and board games we hardly ever saw. I understand the need for punishment, but you got to draw the line somewhere.

Omega's guards were very physical. They would beat the living crap out of you. Take downs, hand and leg restraints and a restraint chair were used not just for discipline but to punish us. And I spent a lot of time in solitary confinement. That was a living hell, especially when you are a teenager and your mind is developing and you crave exercise. Solitary confinement destroys your mind. You want to create hate, then that's what you do.

So I fought back any way I could. I spit on people, I would bang my head against the walls, threaten to hurt the staff and even their children, curse and scream to create a disturbance, even try to bite the guards who were restraining me. They would take me to the floor for the slightest thing, even if I just raised my hand or wanted to ask a question. They often pepper sprayed me and other boys right in our faces.

Midway through my imprisonment Deputy Penaloza was transferred to Omega, I heard because he was in trouble for gouging a kid's eye out at a boot camp. He was on a total power trip. He thought up new rules, even though he didn't have the authority to do so, but our program director, Sgt. Berg, had been called up to active duty in Iraq, so Penaloza got away with a lot. For some reason, he targeted me.

It started small. He would signal me out for snide remarks or make jokes at my expense. Then he would accuse me of stuff I didn't do. One morning he was outside creeping around the cell windows trying to catch boys breaking the rules, like sleeping or talking. I saw him standing at my window and I just shrugged my shoulders. He radioed to the other guards that I was sleeping and that made me so mad that I flipped him off and got so angry that I convinced the guards that he was a liar.

Things came to a head that afternoon. We were at rec doing exercises when he pointed at me and said I had not been doing pushups like the others, so we would all have to start over. "Bullshit," I said. "You're a lying piece of shit." He got in my face and said I was going to "alternative training" right away. That is a sand and mud box that they flood with water and make you exercise and crawl around in. I grabbed the fence and he tried to pull me off it by holding my wrist and twisting it until I let go. Another guard heard my screams and yelled to Penaloza, "What the fuck are you doing?" They took pictures of my swollen, black and blue wrist and one deputy encouraged me to file an abuse complaint.

Penaloza was sent to work at the county jail. I heard he was busted soon after for bringing cocaine to inmates and then became a fugitive from justice. Fitting.

I was on suicide watch a lot. I became more aggressive. If I could get hold of a paper clip, I'd cut the inside of my mouth and try to spit blood at the guards. If I didn't call a guard "Sir," it was considered disrespectful and I was punished. I *had* no respect for those guards; how could I call them "Sir"? Motherfuckers was what they were, and I told them so. I hit another kid with a broom, and I knew I needed to be written up for that. And probably for making a shank out of a metal binder, toilet paper roll, tape and pencil, to be used to defend myself. But for sleeping in my cell? For asking questions? For wanting to talk to people? Getting kicked in the back and taken to the floor? That's pure punishment.

I learned how to make the most with very little. When they refused to give me another book to read, I bit my lip and spit the blood on the walls of my cell. The guard gave me a bucket full of water and bleach to clean the walls and I threatened to drink the bleach water. At least that got me taken to the psych unit. But nothing ever happened there.

They used different color epaulets to reward progress. I went from red to green, then demoted to red, back to green, then to blue, then demoted to green, back to blue, then orange, then beige, then demoted all the way back to red. Midway through my stay at Omega, a kid named Castro and I admitted we wanted to escape from the program. Who wouldn't! Although it was impossible to escape. But for just saying that, we were put in black and white striped uniforms and handcuffed and shackled when outside of our cells.

My treatment team wrote "no change" in my therapy, year after year. Yet I was doing well in the educational classes and was told I could have graduated early, but they wanted me in a class where I did so well. Maybe because I knew I was close to being discharged, I made it back to beige epaulets before I was released.

I'm not telling this completely from memory. I requested my Omega records once I got to state prison and I have had a chance to review them. I felt angry and sad reading them. I wish that I could have told my side of each incident report. I wish I'd had more classes, maybe even college courses, and more books. I love to read. At Omega, I had to make myself read slowly as I never got enough books.

Looking back, I don't see how I endured Omega. When I learned that it was closed down by the State of Florida, I felt happy, sort of; but I wish I'd been the one who caused it to be closed, like I wish that I had shut down Tony Bryant's foster home, not other abused boys, years later.

State prison is different. Family and friends can visit. I have regular access to the phone, canteen and a lot of athletic activities. For the most part, if you follow the rules the guards leave you alone. They don't taunt you like they did at Omega, telling me that my grandmother gave me back to the state after she adopted me because I was so terrible. And not telling me for months that my grandmother died.

How do you train a pit bull to fight? Put it in a cage and never show it love or affection. The only contact is to harass it and poke and prod. When you release it, it's ready to fight. Well, that's Omega.

I read in the Omega reports that I had some kind of evaluation when I was eighteen. The person wrote: "Youth's behavior is terrible. Youth has been in the program for 43 months. This program has done everything possible to change this youth's behavior. Needs to go to adult prison as there is no hope for change."

Well, here I am in prison. But who robbed me of any hope for change?

Chapter 7

Letter Written from Florida State Prison
February 3, 2012

Dear Judge Sullivan,

You asked me to write more about my time in solitary confinement at Omega Juvenile Prison, what I did to pass the time, what it was like to be locked up alone for days and nights and weeks at a time. I told you it was too painful for me to do. You said I could write it like a story, like fiction, so I thought about it and here is what I wrote. I'm not bragging about it. I'm pretty much a self-taught writer.

Alpha & Omega:

Suddenly I found myself flying toward the floor. One minute I was nice and snug in my dreams...free. The next I was rudely awakened by shouts and kicks. The abruptness of it had me confused. Why is this happening? What have I done? Where am I?

"Get on the wall! Face the fucking wall!"

"Looks like we got one who thinks this is the Holiday Inn, Sarge."

"What the fuck are you looking at? Eyes on the fucking wall and don't let me see you move again."

My head is smacked from behind with enough force to bounce it off the wall and leave me dazed. The unfairness of it breaks something from within. I begin to turn towards my attackers in a mounting rage, but only make it halfway before I'm flying towards the floor once again. Three grown men land on top of me. One shoves his knee into my back, pushing my face into the concrete while grabbing my arm and twisting at the same time. Someone has my arm bent at an impossible angle.

As if that's not enough, the sarge sprays me in the face with a can of pepper spray. I can't see or breathe. The burning is unbelievable. I begin to gag but can't even find a little air to choke on because some 200-lb goon's got all his weight pressed into my back forcing all the air out of my stomach. After all, I'm 4'11" and 89 pounds.

The guards laugh and make some comments I don't catch. I'm still looking for air. I begin to cry.

The guards laugh even harder at that. "Jesus, we got a fucking crybaby. Not just some big bad thug, are you now? Just a little punk. That's what you are from now on. You understand me, punk?

I cry silently, trying to hold back the tears and ashamed of myself for showing any weakness. Come on man, get it together, I coach myself. Shit yours is now. This ain't nothing noways, you've dealt with way worse. What's with the tears? You want people to think you're weak?

Still, it takes a while to catch ahold of my emotions. The unfairness of it assaults me, and it's like the leaves of a dam have been flung wide open. Why? Why??

"What I do?" I manage to squawk.

"Shut up! No one gave you permission to talk."

What type of crap is this? I haven't done nothing, and I can't seem to do nothing right.

"Am I fucking talking to myself? Did I just address you?"

"Huh? I'm confused. Shut up or what? Which do you want?"

"Sir, yes sir or no sir when I ask you a question punk!"

"Sir?"

"Sir yes sir!"

"Sir yes sir." I think I'm going to cry again but I'm starting to get so mad that my anger helps me fight off a fresh batch of tears.

That was just the beginning. I had just been committed to a juvenile prison. I didn't know that when the lights come on, I was supposed to jump straight out of bed. How was that supposed to wake me up if I'm asleep under the covers? I didn't know when a guard pops my door I have *to run to the wall and stand facing it at attention. I didn't know one could matter so little, that because you were no one and had no one, the state and its minders could do whatever they wanted to you. But I was about to find out.*

I was strong, though. Hell, I'd been through some shit a time or two. This was nothing. At first, anyways.

My days started at 5:00 a.m. I had to get up, get dressed, make my bed and be reading my handbook by 5:15. If not, well, like Sargent Lance used to say, "It's party time." The sick bastard enjoyed putting his hands on us.

I don't know why I had to get up, though. It wasn't like I was going anywhere. I ate in my cell. I was supposed to go to school, but more often than not school was canceled. When it wasn't canceled, they'd just slide a piece of paper under the door and tell us it was our assignment for the day. Man, sleep would have been a lovely escape. I didn't have nothing but a concrete bunk and a pencil and paper to write to my friends and family. What friends? What family? So I had nothing to do.

"Hey, cell 2, cell 2...new guy, come to your vent."

"Yeah, what's up?

"Man, not so loud...you got to whisper. We ain't allowed to talk homey. Where you from?"

"St. Pete."

"Yeah, listen. You just got here so they gone be real hard on you for a while. But it will get better. Just lay low."

"They ever let us out our cell to watch TV, rec or anything?"

My vent rings with the sound of laughter. "What's so funny?"

"Man, listen little bro, you really don't know where you are do you? TV? Are you crazy? You won't come out that cell for a couple months anyways, cause you're new, and when you finally do come out it will probably be to sweep or mop the floor and then right back to your cell."

"But what about school?"

"Maybe sometimes but they almost always cancel."

"I thought they got to let us out for a least an hour a day, like for rec or something?"

"Yeah, they supposed to, but look you don't want to go to no rec

cause it ain't no rec. They going to P.T. your ass raw and that's it."

"P.T.? What's P.T.?"

"Physical training, in other words exercise till you drop. But don't worry, the guards are lazy so they seldom do it, unless they are pissed off or something. And when they have inspections. When Q.A. comes, it's a whole nother world here."

"Man, they just leave us in our cells all day? Can I at least get a book or something?"

"Nope, none of that any time soon. If you don't get in any trouble for about six months, maybe."

"Six months! Man, I'll go crazy by...."

"What the hell are you doing on my vent? Get your ass down!"

I nearly jump out of my skin. A guard has crept down the hall and caught me talking on my vent.

"Oh, so you like to socialize, do you? Well, we will just have to pull you out later tonight and get acquainted, now, won't we?"

I spend the whole day worrying about what "get acquainted" means. Lunch comes. Lunch goes. Same for dinner. I can't lay or sit on my bed. Not allowed till lights out. So I pace back and forth. I'm assaulted with thoughts of what was, what could have been. But I push these regrets away, no time to dwell on the past. Instead, I'll focus on the future. Hell, I can do this "program." I'll get out and start over. This time I'll be an adult, my own man and not have to worry about going to some screwed up foster home or shelter. I'll get a job, go to college, and show all these motherfuckers I'm someone, somebody. Yeah, I'll show them.

Time drags by. The lights go out and I breathe a sigh of relief. They forgot, or must have just been trying to scare me. I can go to bed now, and tomorrow I'll be up early and avoid any mistakes.

Then the door rolls. Standing there is the officer who caught me talking earlier.

"It's time for your education. Follow me," he says.

When it's over I limp back to my cell. I ease myself into bed. And in the quiet, I cry. Gone are the thoughts of college and a job. All that's left is hate. Hate for everyone and everything. But, no matter what you do, how long you keep me caged, one day you will have to release me. One day I'll *be free again. And then you'll be sorry. You will be sorry you ever did that to me. I cry now, but you'll be the one crying later.*

———————

By Leo Boatman, Written at Florida State Prison, February 3, 2012.

Chapter 8

Author's Note

When Leo sent me most of his official file from Omega Juvenile Prison, I couldn't read it in one sitting. It wasn't the length that bothered me so much. It was the extent and depth of abuse that occurred during the years of his imprisonment.

Juvenile judges throughout Florida were recognizing the harm caused by boot camp-style punishment on adolescents. There were national movements led by prominent child psychologists and others to end solitary confinement of adolescents and teenagers who were locked up. As Leo put it, if you want to create a wild animal, lock a boy in a cell with nothing to do and no one to talk to for days at a time.

Experts in the area of teenage behavior and brain development produced proof that a human brain is not fully mature or developed until the age of twenty to twenty-five. What occurs during those brain-development years may well determine the kind of person a youth may become: responsible, empathetic, and kind, or irresponsible, impulsive and cruel.

Leo's foster home experience was inexplicably cruel, amounting to torture that state welfare agencies knew about and repeatedly (and tragically) ignored.

To the best I could determine, Leo Boatman never received a visit from a child welfare case worker during the years he was imprisoned at Omega. He was still a foster child. The law required that visits occur. His family rarely visited. His only human contact was other imprisoned youth and the guards, just a few of them acting kindly.

There was no planning before his release from the prison

shortly after his nineteenth birthday.

This omission, particularly when he was transitioning out of Omega to live on his own, set in motion the events that followed.

66

Chapter 9

Release from Omega and Move to Clearwater
Five Months of Freedom

I was released from Omega in August 2005, a month after my nineteenth birthday. The state lost jurisdiction to hold me in a juvenile facility. The last entry made on my chronological record at Omega says, "Youth released from program to parents." Hah! That shows how little Omega really knew or cared about me.

The chaplain at Omega took me to my sister's apartment off Highland Avenue and Union Street in Clearwater. They had Rosie's address, although she hadn't visited me in years. We knocked, but no one answered her door. After waiting a while, he gave me twenty bucks and wished me luck. I walked around all day. You can imagine how I felt being free after more than six years locked up!

After a while I went back to my sister's and found that she had been there all along, sleeping, on my big day. But she seemed happy to see me and said I could stay with her for a while—actually with her and her boyfriend Kevin. Kevin smoked a lot of dope. Now don't get me wrong. Kevin was nice to me and treated me well. But he was like anyone else when he smoked pot.

Their apartment had only one bedroom, but it was neat, pretty nice and up to date, furnished with a living room set and a big TV. The kitchen was newish. I slept on a futon in between the kitchen and living room.

I'd been at Omega so long that you think they would have been prepared for my release. I had also aged out of foster care at eighteen while at Omega, and the caseworker should have prepared me at that time. I don't even remember a visit from a foster care caseworker all the years I was at Omega. As it was, when I got out, I had no ID. No social security card, no birth certificate, nothing. I spent about a month trying to prove who I was. The only reason I got the independent living checks, about $850 a month, for aging out of foster care, was because I researched the new program before I left Omega. I pulled it off the website, as well as enrollment information from St. Petersburg College. What Omega gave me was—the boot!

I liked getting to know Rosie again, and staying with her and her boyfriend was fine for a short time. We went to the beach, to fast food places that I liked and hadn't been to in six years. It was fun just hanging around. I told Rosie about the $850 a month I was getting from the state as an independent living stipend, and suddenly things changed. She said she'd been caught driving without a license a few times and had racked up serious charges: three misdemeanors and a felony. She was released on her own recognizance and said she needed $3,000 to hire a lawyer for the court hearing and didn't have the money. I gave her two checks for $500 each and found out later that she gave the money to her drug-dealing boyfriend. That did it for me.

Rosie did give me a place to stay and bought some food, but two months with her was enough. She was too motherly, asking where I'd been, complaining about the late hours I kept. It got annoying. So I asked to move in with my Uncle Vic, who had just been released from prison again after serving time on drug charges.

In the meantime I caught up with some old friends from school and from my grandmother's neighborhood. Ricky Watts was my best friend. I was so happy to see him. He worked at a fancy restaurant, the Island Way Grill, in Clearwater. Other friends, Steven, Josh, Joe and Adrienne all got together with me and accepted me back into the fold. They were true friends and didn't talk about the past. Sometimes I'd do something stupid or say something weird, but then I'd just say, "Dude, I've been locked up for six years," and we'd laugh. They let me drive their cars sometimes, and we'd laugh at my mistakes. I learned pretty quickly, though.

And the girls. Oh boy. After being locked up for six years, you can imagine what it was like to discover girls, actually women by now. The first one I had sex with was Amanda, a 5'4" blonde, very cute, working as a telemarketer. I'd had a crush on her when I was twelve. She was my best friend Ricky's younger sister. We hit it off again shortly after my release from Omega. I guess it was shared passion, and it was my first time with a woman. It confirmed what I already knew: I *always* preferred women. But it began to get awkward because of Ricky, so we broke it off.

Stephanie Lopez was the next girl I dated. She was a waitress at the Hooters restaurant where I worked. She was about my age, very small, about 5'1", 115 lbs., with long, dark, curly hair. She was bright, friendly and smart and from Puerto Rico. Hooters hires the waitresses because of their looks, and she was definitely in the top two of the prettiest girls there. She took me to parties given by her friends. Boy, could she eat, for such a little thing. We had sex but she had a steady boyfriend, so she ended it with me. Then there was Cynthia, 5'6", older and single, a dancer at Baby Dolls. That was only a one-night stand, like with another, Stephanie, a redhead who worked at Pete and Shorty's restaurant. Her boyfriend was in the Pinellas County jail. I didn't really complain when they had boyfriends. What the heck...

Looking back, maybe I should never have left my sister Rosie's apartment. Maybe the bad stuff wouldn't have happened. After all, I had forgiven Rosie for taking my independent living money and giving it to her pothead boyfriend. But she started acting like a mother.

"Where are you going, Leo? Why were you out so late last night? What time are you coming home? What are you doing with your money?"

"Bitch, bitch, bitch," I'd tell her. I didn't leave Omega to have my sister crimping my wings. I wasn't a kid. I wanted independence. I wanted freedom. Uncle Vic could provide that, I thought. He was married to Aunt Joy, but that didn't last long, and he was alone again.

Vic had a little tin can of a trailer. I moved in with him. He basically didn't give a damn what I did as he was just released from prison and was enjoying his freedom as much as I was. Vic charged me $300 a month for half the $600 he said it cost him to live in his trailer. It really was a crappy place, but I had a full-time job at Hooters—the original, first Hooters in Clearwater, the restaurant famous for re-inventing chicken wings served by sexy waitresses wearing skimpy outfits. My cousin Tiffany Price got me the job. She got Vic one too. She worked there as a waitress.

Now for a 19-year-old guy who just spent six years locked up, you couldn't pick a better restaurant to bus tables at. Hooters was started by some businessmen from Clearwater who wanted to bring Buffalo-style chicken wings to Florida with a little pizzazz. The restaurants had big indoor and out-door bars, pine paneling and large screen TVs for the sports crowd. Best of all, the waitresses were sexy as hell, pretty good looking but with knockout figures. They wore tight little orange shorts and tight white tank tops. The customers were mostly men, although some women and families came too. The wings tasted great. You could get them breaded, bone-less, blackened, naked or sauced. The sauces ranged from mild and medium to hot, classic barbeque, honey Thai pepper and so on. The wings were washed down with pitchers of icy cold beer. The people who worked there and the customers were friendly. The waitresses flirted with everyone.

The restaurant held an annual worldwide wing eating contest each year. I think the winners gobble up more than 150 wings in ten minutes. Anyway, I took pride in my job as a busboy and dishwasher, as well as the fact that I was earning money to support myself. I only missed work once in those three or four months. I was well liked by the waitresses and the kitchen help. I was paid $7.50 an hour. It was the first real job I'd ever had. I felt like I was really getting my stuff together after all those years locked up.

"Vic, with my $850 stipend from the state and my Hooters money, we can move into something better than this trailer after the first of the year," I said. "I think I've found something for just ten dollars more a month."

"Keep an eye on it," Vic told me. "I'm not in love with this dump either."

College tuition and books were free, so if I kept my job at Hooters, I was sure we could swing it. I felt good about that, being able to help old Uncle Vic get a decent place to live. I had even met a nice lady from the independent living agency. Her name was Hope and she gave me left over vouchers for clothes, so I didn't have to spend money on that. Things were definitely looking up.

Vic and I made friends with Nick, a cook at Hooters. Vic's friend Lucas took all of us to the Round Up in Oldsmar. It was basically a bar with a huge square dance floor that featured a hip hop/techno night. That was kind of funny because you've got these big country boys in shit-kicker cowboy hats as bouncers and a bunch of young people dancing to hip hop in the midst of flashing strobe lights.

"Let's dance," I said to Cynthia, the stripper I dated for a while. We were dancing up a storm as Lucas and Nick got into a drinking competition. Nick started to hang on Luke's shoulder, slobbering, while Luke said he was just getting started and downed another shot.

"Gimme the car keys, Luke," I asked, and he was so drunk that he did it.

"Let's go, Cynthia," I said, grabbing her hand. So Cynthia and I were in the back seat making out when Vic and Luke opened the car and yelled to "haul ass." They threw Nick into the back seat and we drove off, tires squealing. They told us that the biggest bouncer tried to separate Nick and Luke, and Nick faked making a pass at him.

"Those other assholes had to hold the big guy back while we cleared out of the place," Vic laughed.

Nick threw up in the car. What a mess. To get back at him we asked him questions like "what color panties are you wearing?" and then recorded his answers on our cell phones to torment him when he got sober. Cynthia, Vic and I hadn't had anything to drink and were trying to help Nick when we got back to Vic's house, but he crawled over to the street and wanted to lay there. A neighbor came out with a bottle of Jack Daniels and a joint. We passed both around as we looked at Nick still lying in the street.

"Hey," Vic said to the neighbor. "Can you find us a pen or crayon or something?"

We laughed when he brought us a black Magic Marker. We all started drawing crude pictures over Nick's body. I took pictures of him while everyone else lined up and mooned the camera.

"Let's find a motel," Cynthia said, rubbing up against me.

"I don't have any money for a motel," I told her. "But I have a better idea. Sex on the beach is supposed to be more romantic."

Well, it's not all it is cracked up to be. Sand gets everywhere and we almost got caught. Cynthia went home when we finished, and I went to work. There was Nick standing over a hot grill looking like hell with red marks all over his body where the pictures had been. Apparently he got home and passed out in bed, where his mother found him. When she saw the drawings, she threatened to kick him out of the house if he didn't scrub them off and get to work.

Freedom, hanging out, going to the beach, McDonald's, laughing, hanging out with friends, people smiling at you, ordinary people being nice to you. Job at Hooters, original, dishwasher, kitchen, nice people. Earning money, wishing to get out of tin can, being productive, nice people at work, meeting more all the time, met a girl, sort of dates, sex. Sounds routine to many at 19, but not to me. New and different sights, sounds, smells sensations. The ordinary was wonderful. People nice and helpful, no shouting, no one mean. I thrived at work, with friends. I was looking forward to starting St. Petersburg College in January. I still wanted to be a veterinarian technician. They had a good program for it at the college. I wanted to work with a real veterinarian, and I wanted to get a dog of my own, too. I had a lot of things to look forward to, considering how bad the last six years had been.

In the fall of 2005, Vic and I visited some distant relatives who lived out in the country, somewhere in Central Florida. I rode on the back of his motorcycle to their home for a big barbeque. They owned small dirt bikes with motors, and before long I was keeping up with Vic on his motorcycle. I had the dirt bike going full speed, doing spins and circles, almost laying it down. Vic was surprised how fast I caught on to riding it. We howled and hooted and gunned those bikes for miles up and down the country roads.

Someone had a rifle at the barbeque, an assault weapon. I'd never shot one before. Vic set up some targets in the wooded area—tin cans, cardboard signs and so on—and I practiced shooting the rifle. Like with the dirt bike, I learned pretty quickly.

That Halloween, Vic and I catted around and met up with some folks at a party in the woods. Beer, pot, girls. Your typical party for a couple of horny guys. I'd been out of Omega Juvenile Prison a little more than three months at that point. I was smoking six to seven joints a day, bought with money I earned at Hooters. I thought it relaxed me and made me less angry. But I really don't know. I do know that I was smoking more and more.

Looking back at those months, I think I was the happiest I had been since way back when living with Greg. And then I got angry again.

Chapter 10

8 Big Mistakes in Oversight by Agencies
Analysis by Dewey Caruthers, CEO Caruthers Institute

Boatman's life growing up was a constant series of mistakes in system oversight. Below are the eight biggest ones. Dangerously, many national and state experts in child welfare, foster care and juvenile justice believe the same mistakes in oversight are happening with today's children.

Mistake #1: Conceived and born in a mental institution and father unknown

Mistake #2: Allowed to live with mom till age 4

Mistake #3: Living with grandma, mom and boyfriends

Mistake #4: Allowed to live with Uncle Vic, former felon who served time in prison

Mistake #5: Foster care with Tony

Mistake #6: Sent straight to San Antonio Boys Village—a Level Six, moderate-risk juvenile commitment prison—without ever being given probation

Mistake #7: Transferred to Sago Palm Academy—a level eight, high-risk, juvenile residential facility—without mental health counseling for nine months

Mistake #8: Transferred to Omega Juvenile Prison, a military-style boot camp that used solitary confinement and withheld library books from him

Bonus Mistake: Released from six years of juvenile prison—no halfway house, no probation officer, nor any other oversight

Experts in juvenile justice, foster care and child welfare were surveyed to gain insight into whether the same eight mistakes could happen today, nearly 20 years later, with other children. Shockingly, the survey results show experts agreeing many of the same big mistakes that shaped Leo into a serial killer are happening today.

Mistake #1: Conceived and born in a mental institution and father unknown

Leo Boatman was born in 1986 in G. Pierce Woods State Mental Hospital, an institution in Arcadia, Florida, for individuals with special needs and mental illness. His mother, Sheila Boatman, was a patient who became pregnant after being raped by another patient or a guard.

Years later, in 2002, the state shut down the hospital claiming to save money, but it followed a years-long series of incidents where patients died or were severely abused. A U.S. Department of Justice investigation was pending at the time of closure.

The majority of experts, 81%, believe it is possible in today's mental institutions for a female patient to be raped and become pregnant. Also, if the woman would not identify the rapist, the father would never be known—as was the case with Leo.

One expert commented: "Predators exist in all industries. Patients in mental health institutions are at greater risk, in part because they are less likely to be believed due to their mental health histories. Most institutions are also known to cover up occurrences of rape and pregnancy."

Another added: "I used to work in a psychiatric hospital. I could see how it would be possible for a staff person to gain the trust of the victim and have the opportunity to sexually assault her/him. I also know there were times when staff were not vigilant about monitoring patients, and the victim could, willingly or not, have had sex with another patient."

Mistake #2: Allowed to live with mom till age 4

Shortly after birth Leo was allowed to live with his mom, who was a recent patient at a mental institution. She had been admitted in part because she was incapable of taking care of herself. Upon her release from the institution, she took custody of Leo.

For four years, Leo's mom and her various boyfriends sexually abused him and his older sister. This included one boyfriend taking nude, pornographic photos of Leo and his sister. At age 4, Leo was removed from his mom's home by the Florida Department of Children and Families.

Experts disagreed in the same percentages over whether it is possible today the courts would grant custody of a baby to a mother with a history of serious mental illness that is not being managed. Nearly 40% thought it could happen today, with the same percentage disagreeing. The remaining 25% said, "I don't know/don't want to answer."

One expert commented: "I feel this situation would be rare today. If anything, the courts may place custody with a parent who is mentally ill if that parent also resided with someone who could support them, such as a grandparent or other family member."

<u>Mistake #3: Allowed to live with grandma, mom and boyfriends</u>

After the Florida Department of Children and Families removed Leo and his older sister from their mom's home, custody of the children was assigned to the grandmother, Sheila's mom. Shortly after, the grandmother allowed Sheila to move into her home. Sheila and various boyfriends sexually molested Leo and his sister on a regular basis.

A large majority, nearly 90%, think the Florida Department of Children and Families today could allow, even by mistake, a mom who just lost custody of her child to live under the same roof again. Six percent disagreed and another six percent did not know/did not want to answer the question.

Additionally, nearly 90% believed it is possible today that the Florida Department of Children and Families would not be able to detect ongoing sexual abuse and molestation of very young children. No one disagreed, but 13% did not know/did not want to answer the question.

An expert explained that young children don't know or understand what's happening to them is wrong, unable to differentiate abuse from loving attention. "Often abuse is discovered by an innocent remark from the child, they don't know that they just described abuse. For example, an eight-year-old client of mine casually mentioned about 'when she takes showers with her father' without realizing that would raise lots of questions."

One expert identified this as a regular occurrence today: "This is all too common. I have seen this situation come up in court many times. The child welfare system is overwhelmed with little funding or support. Kids slip through the cracks all the time." Another expert agreed: "Unfortunately relatives do allow biological parents to move back in without informing case managers."

A couple of experts focused on the pay, experience and training of case workers. "Many case workers are inexperienced and children have been trained to cover up home problems," one said. The other added: "Due to the lack of pay and training and oversight, sadly shortcuts and mistakes are made."

Mistake #4: Allowed to live with Uncle Vic, former felon who served time in prison

The state later allowed Leo to live with his Uncle Vic (mother's half-brother), a felon recently released from prison. A few years later, Uncle Vic was required to register as a sex offender.

More than 40% of experts disagreed the courts today would grant custody of a child to a convicted felon recently released from prison. However, nearly 30% think it could happen today, with an equal amount responding they did not know/did not want to answer the question.

Two experts viewed being a convicted felon as an automatic disqualifier: "Conviction and prison would be a disqualifier," one expert commented. Two other experts believed it could happen today based on the type of felony. "It all depends on what the uncle was convicted of."

Additionally, most experts, 80%, think the Florida Department of Children and Families today, even by mistake, could allow a child to live with a family member who is a convicted felon recently released from prison.

Mistake #5: Foster care with Tony

After a short-term confinement via a Baker Act due to suicidal and dangerous behaviors, Leo was sent to a foster home run by Tony, who specialized in handling the most out-of-control kids. Tony's foster home included housing six boys, some intellectually disabled and emotionally disturbed, in the same bedroom with two bunk beds and a folding bed in the middle. The younger foster kids were physically and sexually abused by an older foster child.

Additionally, during this time Leo and the other children were physically, mentally and emotionally abused by Tony, who made them get naked and do jumping jacks until their feet were swollen and bloody. The DCF case manager assigned to the foster home did not believe the allegations made by Leo and the other foster kids. Tony's foster home was later closed after abuse allegations were finally verified.

The majority of experts, 80%, believe it is possible children in today's foster homes could be repeatedly abused, physically and sexually, over years by a foster parent without Florida Department of Children and Families detecting the abuse. Only seven percent think it cannot happen today, with the remaining 13% saying they did not know/did not want to answer the question.

A few experts identified the issue of foster care agencies more often believing foster parents than foster children. "Children with problematic backgrounds who report abuse are minimized or said to be lying," one commented. Another added: "Often children with histories of behavioral problems are not believed—more often than not the adults are believed."

One expert focused on the challenge of identifying unverified abuse: "To be fair, it is hard to verify abuse if there are no marks. And typically, I have seen that in the absence of evidence, usually the adults are believed, and the kids are seen as acting out. (And sometimes the kids are.)"

<u>Mistake #6: Sent straight to San Antonio Boys Village— a Level Six, moderate-risk juvenile commitment prison—without ever being given probation.</u>

Leo frequently ran away from his foster home run by Tony. While at Tony's, Leo also committed numerous crimes in a short span, including auto theft, possession of a concealed weapon and arson of a restaurant.

For the crimes, Leo was never given probation, nor ever provided the services of a probation officer, to help improve his behavior. Rather, for his crimes Leo was sent straight to San Antonio Boys Village, a juvenile commitment program.

An expert commented: "Leo never had the benefit of a juvenile probation officer, which could have changed his life and saved the lives of his victims in the Ocala National Forest."

The same expert explained juvenile probation: "Juvenile probation focuses on the root cause of why the youth committed the offense. It takes a balanced approach to justice, looking at accountability, community safety and competency. With this evidence-based approach, the youth is held accountable, the community is safe with a curfew and monitoring by the juvenile probation officer and competencies are addressed through community agencies that assist in treating delinquent behaviors."

Nearly three-quarters of experts think it is possible today for a child to be sent directly to a juvenile commitment program without first being given a probation officer to help improve his/her behavior. "DJJ and SAO may feel certain children need higher levels of supervision for public safety," an expert said.

Mistake #7: Transferred to Sago Palm Academy— a level eight, high-risk, juvenile residential facility— without mental health counseling for nine months

After escaping twice from San Antonio Boys Village, Leo was transferred to Sago Palm Academy for high-risk children. During this time, he was sexually molested by a cell mate. Leo also was encouraged by the guards to fight other juvenile inmates.

In his initial nine months at Sago Palm Academy, Leo was not provided any mental health treatment, such as counseling and therapy. The mental health services later provided grief counseling, due to the death of his grandmother.

All of the experts agreed—the only occurrence of 100% agreement in the survey responses—that it is possible in today's juvenile prisons for an inmate to be sexually assaulted by his cell mate. Many cited lack of supervision for the widespread sexual assaults. "Lack of appropriate supervision is commonplace," one expert said.

Additionally, nearly three-quarters think in today's juvenile prisons that guards encourage fighting among inmates. The remainder disagreed.

"Guards sometimes encourage this type of behavior or at least don't care enough to stop it. They are hired to keep kids in line, not to actually support and help them," an expert commented. "I think all sorts of scary things happen at facilities, to girls and to boys. Periodically I come across new stories about these incidents," another expert added.

Moreover, the majority of experts, 86%, think it is possible in today's juvenile prisons that an inmate can be admitted and not receive mental health services for nine months. Seven percent disagreed and another seven percent cited they did not know/did not want to answer the question.

Mistake #8: Transferred to Omega Juvenile Prison, a military-style boot camp that used solitary confinement

At Sago Palm Academy, Leo was repeatedly in trouble, which he did intentionally to get transferred to a safer facility. However, his actions unexpectedly landed him in Omega Juvenile Prison, a military-style boot camp that utilized solitary confinement for discipline.

The prison's culture accepted violence between guards and juvenile inmates, which in part later led to the banning of boot-camp institutions in Florida. During his time, Leo joined a prison gang and was regularly involved in violence. Additionally, he was placed in solitary confinement frequently for many days at a time, without the benefit of the books he requested. How callous and counterproductive that was! At age 19, he was released as the state lost jurisdiction over him.

Experts were asked an open-ended question: What are today's juvenile prisons using in place of solitary confinement since being banned?

While most reported they did not know, one expert reported the only change being supervision by a guard. "Solitary is still being used, except a guard is stationed at the door," an expert commented.

Bonus Mistake: Released from six years of juvenile prison—no halfway house, no probation officer, nor any other oversight

Leo Boatman was released at age 19 with no oversight, which means he did not have transition resources like a halfway house nor a probation officer to regularly check in with him.

Boatman was a loaded weapon ready to fire that was tossed into the general public, and no one was assigned to watch over the danger posed.

The only resource Boatman left prison with was a grant stipend for foster children aging out of care, which he procured himself without any help.

All of this begs the question: What did the State of Florida think was going to happen?

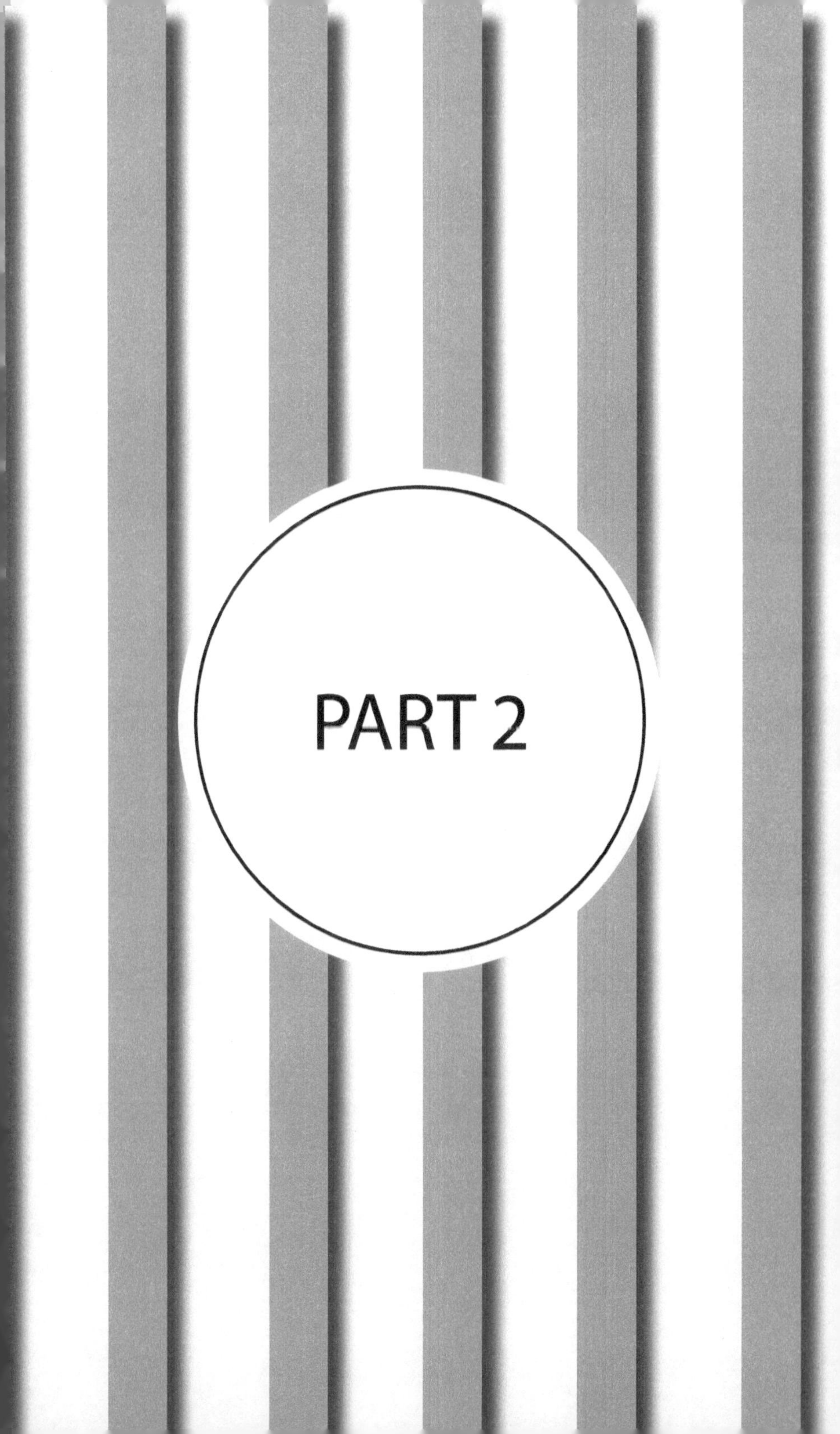
PART 2

Chapter 11

Five Months of Freedom, Finished

I had just about stopped resenting Rosie for taking my independent living money and giving it to her pothead boyfriend. Really, it was much better living with Vic than arguing with Rosie for her trying to control my life. Then, Vic let me down big time. It all involved a motorcycle.

Here I was, nineteen years old and I had never had a driver's license and, of course, I hadn't taken driver's training. They don't offer that at Omega. (Hah!) I had never really driven a car any distance. I was tired of begging for rides or riding the bus in Pinellas County. Trying to get around the county on a bus, or two or three of them, was a joke.

I'd proved to Vic that I was a quick learner. I'd kept even with his motorcycle on that little dirt bike at the barbeque, but I never got to ride it after that. I needed wheels of my own.

So I talked Vic into helping me buy a motorcycle from a friend of ours, Lucas Merryfield. Lucas bought it from Cycle Springs off Highway 19. Lucas didn't have a license yet, so he had Vic drive it to our place. Not even a week later Lucas decided to get back together with his girlfriend up in Ohio. So she moved down with their child, and he had to get a place for all of them to live. Lucas couldn't afford the bike, so I had my Uncle Grant draw up a loan assumption agreement. Basically, I agreed to take over the payments.

That's how, in November of 2005, four months after my release from Omega, I ended up with a brand new 2006 ZR636

Kawasaki Ninja. It was gun metal silver with red flames and red titanium wheels. I even had a real nice helmet that matched, with a red and gray dragon on it. Real nice and flashy. Here it was still 2005 and I've already got a 2006 bike!

The bike's top speed was 185 mph. The fastest I ever went on it was 161 mph, and that was with Vic driving. We were on our way to my uncle's for Christmas and we pulled up to the light right before you cross the Courtney Campbell Causeway. Some guy on a 250cc bike revved up and challenged us. We hit 161 and I was literally sliding off the back. The guy flagged us down because the wind tore open my backpack and Vic's wallet flew out. We spent about an hour going up and down the road looking for it, but all we found was $1 out of $80. Still, some Good Samaritan mailed Vic's wallet to him a month later with everything except the cash.

Vic promised to teach me to ride the bike, but he kept putting it off. He did practice with me on an old Yamaha a couple of times, so I knew the basics, but I still felt like he was dragging his feet because he got to drive it like it was his bike all the time, and I was making the payments. One time I got off work and had to wait two hours for him to pick me up. Then he asked me to wait while he brought his friend to the house and came back and got me. Huh? That really ticked me off. This was my bike, but Vic had total use of it.

But man, when I did ride on the bike, usually behind Vic, it was really a tranquil and free feeling. We would come out of Dunedin's historic district and drive along the Gulf view road at night, just going 30 or 40 mph and looking out at the water. And of course the girls who pulled up and screamed for us to do tricks, like a wheelie. Man, that's one thing I sure do miss. That bike was so awesome.

Every time I reminded Vic of his promise to teach me to ride, he would find some excuse. One weekend I thought for sure he'd do it, and I didn't have to work so it was perfect. I waited for him, but he had this friend in Ft. Myers, and he decided to spend the weekend with him. So once again he broke his promise. Meanwhile, he's getting all the enjoyment out of my bike.

I was so pissed. I didn't ask for much from him. In fact, he needed my $300 a month to live in the stupid little tin can. So I decided to teach myself to ride the motorcycle. I did okay the first few times. I loved the sound of it and the speed. I went faster and faster and, you guessed it, the bike got away from me. I was riding in our neighborhood, off Rosary Road, and came upon a sharp curve around Lake Placid. I was taught to ride on a dirt bike with back brakes. This was a real motorcycle, a street bike with front brakes. I wasn't going that fast, like 30 mph, but it was too fast for the sharp curve. I hit the back brakes, skidded and landed down on my right side, almost into the lake. The back brakes snapped off. I was scraped up and my motorcycle boots were ripped up. That kept me from having a seriously injured foot. I had totaled the bike. Now I had to make payments on a useless piece of junk. It was all Vic's fault.

Rosie and Vic. My family. I was angry at both of them. I started thinking of taking off on my own. I didn't need them, or anyone else. That's what independence was beginning to mean. On my own. Self-sufficient. To hell with them!

I had read books about the first explorers in Florida, and about Daniel Boone and Lewis and Clark. I'd read the Mountain Men series. I had read all the old National Geographic magazines they gave us in class at Omega. Vic and I had camped out a few times. I had never camped alone, but I knew I could do it. I'd been alone in solitary confinement. After that, surviving in the woods would be a piece of cake. Me against the world. Independence. Respect. No one would taunt me now that I was 5'9" and 140 pounds. No one would call me a worthless punk who never knew his father, whose mother molested him and whose grandmother gave him away.

I might even hike the Appalachian Trail sometime. A fellow told me that you could pick it up in the Ocala National

Forest, just a few hours from here. Maybe I should take a look at it, camp out for a few days. I had some time left before college started. I would show them. I would show them that I didn't need them. I'd show them what Leo Boatman could do on his own. I was excited. And I was still so mad at them.

Chapter 12

Looking Back at Baker Acts

I was aware that getting angry at Vic was not a good idea.

Over the years, I had been in and out of psychiatric hospitals and solitary confinement for not being able to control my anger. Vic told me that I "blew" the best placement I could have had when I was eight years old and broke all the toys that my Aunt Regina and her boyfriend Robert gave me. I had emergency treatment and so-called group therapy at Omega, which was a joke, but I can't remember having one professional person sit down and talk to me alone about how I felt for any significant period of time.

As I look back at the mental health treatment I received as a child and then a teenager locked up in juvenile prisons, I know for a fact I didn't understand it at all when I was going through it. Frankly, I can't look back on anything that helped me during those years, let's say from age nine or so to nineteen. Unlike the foster care and juvenile commitment records that I've had a chance to review, the psychiatric records—if any existed—weren't sent to me. So this is, from my memory, the best that I can do.

When my godfather Greg called the caseworker and had me removed from his house after two months because I wanted to watch a movie instead of going upstairs to bed, I was taken to a foster home in Pasco County, to the north of us, and almost immediately Baker Acted (involuntarily committed on a crisis basis) to The Harbor, a mental health facility in Pasco County. I understood that I was admitted because someone thought I was a danger to myself or others. I got out after a couple of days, was placed in the same foster home and Baker Acted again about a month later. When I was released this time, I was placed in another foster home. I remember I had a bow and arrow, and I wouldn't let the foster father in my room. I had the bow drawn back every time he tried to enter, so they Baker Acted me a third time, for longer. I was then placed in a foster home in Pinellas County and quickly ran away. The police found me and Baker Acted me a fourth time, this time at PEMHS in Pinellas County. They released me from PEMHS to Tony Bryant's foster home, which I've told you about. I was ten years old.

I didn't get Baker Acted for the next two years, until I ran from Tony Bryant's home and was placed temporarily in a foster home in Pasco County. I blew up about something, yelled at the foster mom, so they Baker Acted me again (fifth time) at The Harbor. I had a lesion in my throat and ended up at All Children's Hospital in St. Petersburg. I showed my butt to the staff and got Baker Acted again, this time at Morton Plant/ Mease Hospital in Clearwater. They have a small unit way up on the fifth or sixth floor of the hospital. Real fancy. You got to order your own breakfast and have your own shower. This was the sixth time I was Baker Acted.

My seventh time was at PEMHS again, in St. Petersburg. I had run away again and didn't feel like going back, so I told them I was suicidal. That got me a couple of days at PEMHS, away from foster care. Then I got committed on the juvenile charges and sent to San Antonio Boys Village. My final Baker Act occurred there. I caused some trouble and they sent me back to the Harbor again, in Pasco County. I guess they thought I was crazy.

Now in all these places and at all these times, they didn't spend much time talking to me. They shot me up with all kinds of meds. A lot. Ritalin, Adderall, Depakote, Lithium, Clonidine, Prozac, Tegretol, Trazadone and Seroquel. Those last two were really powerful.

As far as counseling, remember that Tony Bryant's foster home was part of Suncoast Mental Health and was supposed to be therapeutic foster care. Maybe that's where I was supposed to get counseling, not 1,000 jumping jacks and screaming.

So, pretty much from age ten on at the Bryants' home and others, I saw a psychiatrist every month I was on medication. Not that I really saw the doctor. I would go into his office. He would look at reports from Tony or whoever and jot down some notes. He would ask if the meds were messing me up, and that was really it. If I told him what was going on at Tony's foster home, he'd ask Tony about it and we'd all be punished when we got back. Tony would yell, "jumping jacks" and we'd all have to perform.

But I was glad to stay out of Baker Acts. In those places they have some cells they call "time out rooms." In the room is a four-point bed they strap you to. It's like being tied to a concrete bed in a dungeon. They leave you there. This naturally upsets any nine- or ten-year-old boy. When you scream or yell or cry, they tell you to shut up or you will get a shot. The shots make you feel horrible at first and they leave bruises on your butt.

You see some of the craziest things in these Baker Act places. Kids trying to kill themselves, cutting themselves wide open. Schizophrenics who charge walls at full speed and knock out their own teeth. Nobody to really talk to, although by then I didn't expect it.

During the four years I was at Omega Juvenile Prison, I was on a lot of different drugs. When I was released, I wasn't given any medication or prescriptions. Cold turkey. I don't think I noticed any difference.

More recently, as part of my attorneys' work in the Ocala murder case, I was examined by a doctor they chose. He saw me twice for a total of 30 minutes and focused on head injuries I had as a child and, more recently, the fact that my mother supposedly used alcohol and drugs during her pregnancy with me. Wasn't she locked up in a mental hospital?

So what if I was hit in the head with a metal airplane at age five? Pushed against the wall and knocked unconscious by my grandmother at age seven. Tackled by a guard while imprisoned at age thirteen or knocked unconscious by a guard at age seventeen? So what? All boys go through stuff like that. What about the cruel taunting by guards, the days in solitary confinement?

This doctor did hit on one thing that may be important. After I was released from Omega and before the killings, I got into a fight with a friend in a car over a girl in Clearwater Beach. I was clearly drunk and may have been drugged with my friend's Klonopin. My friend kicked me repeatedly in the head and I was taken by ambulance to Morton Plant/Mease Hospital. I was stuck with needles and then snuck out. My sister Rosie said I had a second-degree concussion. I did notice that I was more easily angered after that episode. My sister Rosie and I began fighting again, which is why I moved in with my Uncle Vic. Maybe that concussion and anger did have something to do with what happened. I don't know.

So that's my mental health history, as I remember it. I can count on one hand the people who were nice to me or talked to me kindly in those nine years, from ten to nineteen. I wish there had been more of them. That would have made up for mental health counseling, I think.

Chapter 13

Hidden Pond
January 2–3, 2006

I was still angry with Vic about the motorcycle. I wanted to be by myself, on my own. I had camped a few times years ago with Greg and, more recently, with Vic. I liked everything about camping and wanted to go deep into the woods. I decided to take off on my own before classes began at St. Petersburg College. I chose the Ocala National Forest.

I walked to the Greyhound Bus Station in the late afternoon of January 2, carrying an AK-47 rifle and four boxes of ammo zipped into a long blue nylon bag. The rifle belonged to Lucas Merryfield, the same guy I got the motorcycle from. Lucas said his mother was visiting from Ohio over the holidays, and he didn't want her to find out he had a rifle in his trailer along with his little kid. Lucas called Vic to ask if he could store it at our trailer. Vic told Lucas no, absolutely not. Vic was a convicted felon, and he would go back to prison if found with a weapon in his possession. He wanted no part of that assault rifle.

Lucas then phoned me. He told me what Vic had said, then asked if he could store the rifle in the closet in my bedroom.

"Vic doesn't have to know about the rifle. It's only for a few days. Come on, Leo. I'll make it up to you."

"All right, Luke, bring it over now," I said.

So I took the high-powered rifle with me on my camping trip. Did I ask Vic if I could take it? No. Did I steal it? I don't think so. It was in my closet. I'd seen it at Luke's trailer when he passed it around. I'd used a similar gun for target practice a little while ago. I figured I might find some squirrels or other little critters to hunt while camping. The gun was pretty cool.

I chose the Ocala National Forest because it was easy to get there from Clearwater, only a three-hour bus ride. I had read a little about it and learned that it was the most southern forest in the United States, with thousands of acres of wilderness, rivers, lakes and ponds. Hikers and backpackers seemed to like it because you could get away from people in no time. That suited me fine.

On my way to the bus station, I cashed my independent living check for $875 at Amscot and bought about $17.00 worth of bullets from Deer Hunter Guns. The bus ticket to Ocala cost me $32.50, so I had plenty of money left over for camping supplies and food. I figured I'd get those things closer to the forest.

Once the bus got to Ocala, I took a cab from the bus station to an all-night Walmart. I guessed they would have the camping supplies I needed. I really liked shopping for the stuff I thought I would need. I bought a sleeping bag, tent, backpack, mess kit, knife, binoculars, camp stove and lantern, as well as hiking boots and even a sewing kit. It was a lot of stuff, costing almost $400, but I figured I could use it for other trips, especially if I hiked the Appalachian Trail. I called a cab and asked him to take me and my gear to a nearby campground.

It was the middle of the night when the cab driver dropped me off at Juniper Springs. The gate was locked for the night, so I set up my first camp right outside the gate. I was pretty excited and happy at this point, especially with all my new stuff. I was tired too. I slept for a few hours.

In the morning, after packing up, a worker from the forest came by and gave me directions to a nearby store where I got a lot of food, a map and a disposable camera. That set me back another $150. Who said camping was inexpensive? I felt proud that I could buy everything myself and was looking forward to living on my own.

I set off into the forest, snapping pictures of wildflowers, little critters and crazy big spiders. The tall pines surrounded me, providing shade and making it easier to hike uphill with a full backpack. As I walked, I had time to think. It was so quiet. Like a quiet I'd never experienced. More quiet than solitary confinement, where you could hear the noise of people you couldn't see.

I passed an old couple wearing hardhats and we said hello to each other. They seemed nice and friendly, and I didn't even know them. I knew Tony Bryant. I knew the guards at Omega. Friendly, they were not. I began to think of them. I started daydreaming about Special Forces, about a military lifestyle. I was equipped for anything. I was roughing it, no contact with people. Screw people. Screw the guards who taunted me. Screw Tony Bryant and his fucking jumping jacks. I craved solitude but I hated loneliness. Does that make sense? It would have been nice to be hiking together with someone, to share this experience. That thought made me sad, and angry. I started to get angry at Vic again for the motorcycle.

It was so beautiful in the forest, but somehow I got angrier with each step I took. I wasn't thinking about camping anymore. I was thinking fire, rage, guns, revenge. I was thinking of guards, cells and solitary. Alone. I was alone there and alone here. No one cared a shit about me. No one had or ever would. Some who loved me left me. Some who loved me used me. Alone. I wasn't even certain where I was going. I was headed for Hidden Pond and further. I might be lost, I thought.

I couldn't keep the Omega thoughts away. They took over my head. The guards, the taunts, the beatings. I had power now. I had a rifle. But the guards weren't here. I thought what I might do if I saw a person in a secluded spot. I could kill. I had power.

I saw a man and woman come out of the woods. They looked like a young couple in their twenties. They were talking and laughing. They were taking down their campsite. They asked where I was headed. When I told them, they said I was going the wrong way. They set me right on the directions. They were real nice to me and they seemed happy. I sat down on a hillside and watched them pack up their stuff. They looked so easy and relaxed together.

It was all anger now inside my head. I saw guards walking up the hill. I saw Tony Bryant in the forest. I saw 1,000 jumping jacks. I got out my rifle. The man and woman came past the pond and headed back up the hill where I sat to get the rest of their gear. I aimed my rifle at the man. He saw me and looked startled. I panicked. What if he saw me aiming at him? I had read James Patterson books. I knew what an instant could do. I acted.

I pulled the trigger once, twice. He fell to the ground. The woman screamed. I pulled the trigger again and shot her once. She fell to the ground next to him and kept screaming. I ran closer to her and shot her again...and again...and again...and again.

Chapter 14

The Arrest

Ben Montgomery Story for
the *St. Petersburg Times*

The two murders at Hidden Pond in the Ocala National Forest made headlines across Florida. Law enforcement launched a massive manhunt for the person dubbed "The Forest Killer" by the media. People were horrified that innocent lives could be taken so abruptly and brutally in such a pristine setting.

Leo Boatman finished his first day of classes at St. Petersburg College and was doing homework in the run-down trailer he shared with his Uncle Vic when he was arrested. He had enjoyed his first day in college, telling people he wanted to become a veterinarian technician. He told his Uncle Vic, "I'm really going to like college. It's going to be a piece of cake."

Vic was not happy with Leo or with Lucas. He'd found out about the rifle because Lucas was asking for its return. Vic searched the trailer and couldn't find it. He called Leo on his cell phone. Leo said he was heading home from the forest on a Greyhound bus. He said he had the rifle with him.

"Tell Luke to cool it," Leo said when he got back to the trailer. Vic thought Leo looked terrible, like he'd been in the woods for a while. He stank.

"Here's his precious rifle. You can take it to him."

Vic took the rifle from Leo. It smelled like gunshot. Vic broke it open and found it loaded with bullets. He removed the bullets.

"Damn it, Leo, what did you do? This is a collector rifle.

Luke's never shot it, never loaded it with bullets. He keeps it as a collector's item. He hopes he can sell it for a profit. It's never been fired."

"Well, it's been fired now," Leo said, leaving the room. Vic took the rifle to Lucas and told him Leo had loaded bullets into it and discharged them. He was surprised that Lucas wasn't angry.

"Doesn't matter to me," Lucas told him. "I'm sick of owning that rifle, having to hide it, trying to be a collector. I'm going to get rid of it."

To Vic's surprise, Marion County deputy sheriffs knocked on the door of the trailer close to midnight, anxious to question Leo. They thought they had evidence tying Leo to the murder scene. Vic was shocked. Leo had spent the day at college and gave no sign of distress. Vic hadn't even heard about the murders in the Ocala National Forest.

The sheriff's office had issued an alert after the victims' bodies were found, offering a $5,000 reward for information leading to an arrest and conviction. Almost immediately, they got a call from Joey Tierney, a 20-year-old from Altoona, who remembered picking up a hitchhiker in the forest the day the college students went missing. Tierney knew the woods well and was used to helping people lost in the forest. Tierney said the hitchhiker mentioned carrying a rifle and a hunting knife and asked Tierney to take him to a nearby motel. Tierney said the hitchhiker said he had graduated from college. Tierney provided a description to the sheriff.

At the Silver River Inn in Silver Springs, Florida, sheriffs found that a Leo Boatman matching the description given by Tierney had registered the night in question using a Largo address. He used a driver's license as identification to check into the motel. The sheriffs also obtained a surveillance video from a nearby gas station where the tipster had also taken Leo. Law enforcement entered Leo's Largo residence that night, eager to see if they had their man.

It did not look like it at first.

Leo admitted that he had been camping in the forest and had hitchhiked to the motel. He told them he rode a Greyhound bus home the next day. He said he had wanted to get away to relax, and he took some marijuana with him. He admitted to owning the rifle case. He showed it to them, but the only thing in it was a pellet gun—nothing like the powerful type of rifle used in these slayings. There were no eyewitnesses or fingerprints tying Leo to the murders. The fact that he was camping in the forest didn't make him guilty. And he had spent the day in college classes and was doing homework. They probably had the wrong man.

The sheriff's officers were about to leave when they got a phone call from the officer sent to interview Leo's sister Rosie, who still lived in Clearwater. Rosie told them that Leo was in trouble for stealing an AK-47 rifle from his uncle's friend, Lucas Merryfield, who lived nearby in the Blue Skies Mobile Home Park. Merryfield had left the rifle at Leo's trailer for safe keeping as his mother was visiting, and he didn't want her to know he kept a powerful rifle in the home he shared with his young child.

Rosie's tip was all the sheriffs needed. Authorities arrested Leo in Pinellas County for theft of the rifle. They then transported him to Ocala in Marion County and charged him with the first-degree murders of John Parker and Amber Peck, students at Santa Fe Community College in Gainesville, Florida. Leo was locked up in the Marion County Jail. Merryfield turned over to authorities the AK-47 rifle that Vic had returned to him. Ballistics tests the next day—using a bullet recovered from one of the victims—confirmed a match to the AK-47 rifle.

Leo had been identified as a former foster kid and juvenile delinquent from Pinellas County. He was a "crossover kid," with cases in the child abuse and delinquency sections of Pinellas and Pasco Circuit courts.

Then others started talking. Uncle Vic remembered that

Leo had come home two days before, disheveled and foul with body odor, yelling at him to "tell Lucas to come and get his gun."

A female friend, Briana Ryan, signed a sworn statement saying that Leo told her, "I went out to the woods and killed someone." She said she asked Leo whether he had killed a bum, and that he replied: "I wouldn't kill a bum because they would have nothing to lose. I came across two preppie kids and killed them. I tried to get them to sink in the water, but they wouldn't sink."

Two days after his arrest the police found the local gun store where Leo had purchased the pellet gun. He'd also bought a 22 rifle and put it on layaway. Leo's attempt at cover up had failed. The evidence against him was insurmountable.

The families of John Parker and Amber Peck were living a nightmare. When the two campers had not returned as scheduled, they had reported them in as missing persons. Amber Peck's father and brother-in-law went searching for them and found their bodies halfway submerged in Hidden Pond on Saturday, two days before Leo was arrested. John Parker's father, younger sister, a cousin and brother-in-law also joined in the search that located the bodies. They knew where to look, as Hidden Pond was John's favorite camping site in the forest.

John was a Marine who had worked on helicopter rotors in Afghanistan and gone to college on the G.I. Bill. He had an eight-year-old daughter and a gun collection. He was easygoing and at home in nature. He had been planning this club camping trip for a while. He emailed the Students for Environmental Harmony and followed up with phone calls to club members. Everyone had a conflict except Amber Peck.

Amber was a Michigan transplant who loved nature but hated guns. Her father took her to a range once to teach her to shoot. The two walked out a few minutes later, the girl shaking. She couldn't even pull the trigger.

Amber loved animals. She cried when she saw animals caged at the zoo. She wanted to build a career restoring natural habitats in the wild. Maybe she should become a veterinarian first, she thought. She talked about studying zoology at the University of Florida. She had been accepted for a fellowship at James Cook University in Australia.

Amber was in a hurry that Tuesday morning, getting ready for the camping trip. She told her mother that John was supposed to pick her up and then the two would drive Amber's GMC Jimmy to the forest, park at a trailhead and hike to Hidden Pond.

The discovery of the bodies led to the manhunt and alert, and motorist Tierney's quick response. When the sheriff informed the families of Leo Boatman's arrest, it brought some sense of relief but also the larger question: Why did Leo Boatman do this to their loved ones?

Leo started talking too. Not long after he was put on a "suicide watch" in Marion County Jail, Leo asked Deputy Sheriff Jeff Owens to come to the jail to talk. Despite his public defenders' recommendations not to talk with law enforcement, Leo told Deputy Owens, "I'm more concerned about being on suicide watch in jail." To Leo, it was solitary confinement all over again.

Leo was put on suicide watch at the jail after he tried to take his own life after his arrest, according to jail officials. Leo denied any suicide attempt and said, "I just want to be an inmate. I don't care about a good room and that extra privilege stuff." He admitted to Deputy Owens that he was in the Ocala National Forest-Juniper Run-Hidden Pond area the day the two college students were killed. He told detectives that the shooting was "a spur of the moment" act.

"That's the only thing that, you know, that bothered me about the whole thing," he said.

"What went through your mind to make you shoot these people," a sheriff's investigator asked him.

"I have my little fantasy world and whatnot," he said. "I've read lots of books, you know, and then I probably got onto, like the murder mysteries…They kind of got me into that state of mind." He said he checked John Parker's driver license because he wanted to know who he was. He admitted to partly submerging both bodies in the pond.

He'd confessed, against his lawyers' advice. He allowed a swab sample of his saliva to be taken to test his DNA for matches at the crime scene. Prosecutors were seeking the death penalty.

While awaiting trial in Marion County, Leo was accused twice of making a weapon, a shank, out of a metal strip used as a binder for file folders, which he had sharpened against his metal bunk, wrapped in toilet paper and glued together with dried toothpaste. Once he exchanged the shank for eight Thorazine pills held by another inmate; a second time he alerted officers, the weapon was retrieved, and the other inmate was in trouble.

Marion County jail had a reputation as one of the worst jails in the United States. "Make a shank or be shanked" was inmate scuttlebutt. Leo remained in that jail a year and a half before the trial was scheduled. He wrote the following letter to the *Ocala StarBanner* complaining about conditions in the jail:

"March 9, 2006, 12 a.m.
My name is Leo Boatman and I am an inmate in the Marion County Jail. Since being here I have been denied the rights and privileges of the other inmates. Against my will I have been placed on suicide precaution, even though the head doctor cleared me the jail has kept me on. Twice I have seen doctors with years of experience that think I should not be on S.P. and that I am no harm to myself. This was before and after my recent incident. For the past two weeks I have been chained to the bed in the middle of a dorm. Four of

which I spent four pointed to a bed. I offered no resistance.

They won't allow me to call my family or use the law library, which is very important because of the seriousness of my case. And for some strange reason my friends and family have denied getting any of the letters I've written to them. I eat and sleep in chains. At night I lay awake because of a padlock that is chained in the middle of my back. I'm constantly in a belly chain which my hands are also chained to. My leg is chained to a bed, and I have less room to move around than a dog who is chained up in its own back yard. If I placed someone on a dog leash it would be a civil rights violation, yet there is no difference.

In Iraq we made a big stink about inmates who were put on dog leashes. Well, we do it in our own country because they do it to me. They say it's for my safety, yet they place me with the most violent offenders with no way to protect myself if someone wants to attack me because of my restraints. The higher ups are creating tension between me and inmates who I would otherwise have no problem with.

Because of me they say the other inmates cannot shave or have regular rotations. The only explanation I can think of is they must want to provoke them into attacking me while I am strapped up and defenseless. Why they want to do this would be reasons from anywhere to personal feelings about my case to retaliation for the recent incident. All I know is even the guard who works with me on a daily basis sees no reason for my status but can do nothing because of the higher ups who normally don't get involved with the one-on-one dealing with inmates but have seen fit to be the only ones who make the decisions regarding me.

The jail might say it's for my safety but I'm not

trying to harm myself even though I have plenty of opportunities. They justified the restraints by saying they had to protect the staples in my arm, yet they were removed two days ago and still nothing changed. Some people say this is what I deserve but let me remind you I have yet to be found guilty of anything even if the media painted a different story. Should we change the justice system to punish people before being found guilty? What happened to innocent until being found guilty, and since when is the sheriff my judge and allowed to sentence me?

Shoot, we should just cut the courts out of the whole thing and allow the majors and up to decide what to do with people. It's already obvious to me I have been found guilty so instead of drawing out the torture why don't you just send me to death row and get it over with? Death row is starting to sound better than here, and I would be willing to get there if it's my only other option than staying here. Hopefully this letter will reach you. I've made copies and somehow you will get one. If conditions stay the same, I realize I will not get a fair trial and will just request the state attorney do as he's planning. I would rather be sentenced to death than be chained up like a dog for the rest of my life, forced to eat like one with my hands and wear a woman's dress.
Leo Boatman. Marion County Jail."

Understandably, Leo's letter to the newspaper provoked a lot of response from readers who felt that Leo deserved no better than the conditions he complained of, or maybe worse. Amber Peck's first cousin wrote a blistering response, indicating that Leo would be lucky if he could spend his entire life chained up like a dog, and that a dog didn't deserve a comparison to Leo Boatman.

While Leo and others were complaining about Marion County Jail conditions, others across Florida were taking action against certain Florida juvenile prisons.

Almost the same time Leo was arrested for the murders of John Parker and Amber Peck, a fourteen-year-old African American boy named Martin Lee Anderson died at a Panama City boot camp styled after the boot camps that originated in Manatee County, Florida, home to the Omega Juvenile Prison where Leo was incarcerated.

Martin Anderson died hours after collapsing during a physical exercise regimen that law enforcement officials said is a routine introduction to the boot camp experience. A video of the incident showed the youth collapsing while six to eight guards hovered around him. At least thirteen times, Martin Anderson attempted to rise, sometimes with the officers' help, but each time he fell back to the ground. There is some evidence on the video that the officers may have kneed and punched the youth. A nurse was present and appeared to put a stethoscope to his chest. Attempts to keep the boy walking continued until he slumped to the ground. Paramedics arrived and he was placed on a stretcher and taken to a hospital, where he died a few hours later.

A medical examiner attributed the youth's death not to trauma but to internal bleeding caused by sickle cell trait, a blood disorder not previously diagnosed. An uproar arose throughout Florida. The Bay County sheriff announced he would close down the boot camp. Other boot camps throughout Florida were shut down or voluntarily closed because they felt they couldn't stay in operation without the use of pepper spray and other disciplinary measures.

In October 2007, eight former boot camp workers from the Panama City boot camp were acquitted of manslaughter in the death of Martin Lee Anderson. The defendants testified that they followed the rules at a get-tough facility where young offenders often feigned illness to avoid exercise. Their lawyers said that Martin Anderson died not from rough treatment, but from a previously undiagnosed blood disorder.

Aside from hitting the boy, the guards dragged him around the military-style camp's exercise yard and forced him to inhale ammonia capsules in what they said was an attempt to revive him. The nurse stood by watching.

Defense lawyers argued that the guards properly handled what they thought was a juvenile offender faking illness to avoid exercising on his first day in the camp. He was brought there for violating probation for stealing his grandmother's car and trespassing at school.

The defense said that Martin Anderson's death was unavoidable because he had undiagnosed sickle cell trait, a usually harmless blood disorder that can hinder blood cells' ability to carry oxygen during physical stress.

Prosecutors said the eight defendants neglected the boy by neglecting his medical needs after he collapsed while running laps. They said the defendants suffocated Anderson by covering his mouth and forcing him to inhale ammonia.

The boy's mother, Gina Jones, stormed out of the courtroom. "I cannot see my son no more. Everybody sees their family members. It's wrong," she said, distraught.

"You kill a dog, you go to jail," said her lawyer, Benjamin Crump. "You kill a little Black boy, and nothing happens." He spoke outside the courthouse, which was across the street from the then-closed Bay County boot camp.

Special prosecutor Mark Ober, from Tampa, Florida, said in a statement that he was "extremely disappointed." Then he added, "In spite of these verdicts, Martin Lee Anderson did not die in vain. This case brought needed attention and reform to our juvenile justice system."

Martin Anderson's death led to the resignation of Florida Department of Law Enforcement chief Guy Tunnell, who established the camp when he was Bay County sheriff. Then-governor Jeb Bush had been a strong supporter of the juvenile boot camps, but after Anderson's death he backed the legislature's move to shut down the system and put more money into a less militaristic program.

Omega Juvenile Prison, where Leo Boatman was imprisoned for nearly five years, was closed along with the other boot camps in Florida.

Chapter 15

Plea and Sentence

Author's Note: I followed the pre-trial proceedings for the Ocala Forest murders and talked to Leo and his public defender about them.

Leo's public defender, Bill Miller, prepared him for trial. Statements made by Leo provided enough evidence of pre-meditation for prosecutors to feel justified in seeking a conviction for first-degree murder and a sentence of death by lethal injection. Leo had spoken of wanting to kill the first people he met in the forest. In his videotaped jailhouse confession to Deputy Owens, Leo described how he killed the two college students and then explained how his five years at Omega Juvenile Prison had changed him: "I used to think stuff like that was appalling, you know...I'm not saying like I don't care emotional wise or I don't have emotions or what not. I'm just saying I don't feel them like I should."

There were plenty of emotions from the victims' families.

John Parker was an ex-marine who had served two tours in Afghanistan. He had a six-year-old daughter who lived with her mother in Gainesville. He was studying forestry at the community college and planned to transfer to the University of Florida. He was looking forward to an internship in the Smoky Mountains in North Carolina.

"The woods of the Ocala National Forest were part of his back yard," said his mother, Vicky Parker. She described her family's terrible memories from discovering the victims' bodies.

"How does a father forget seeing his firstborn son lying dead in the water?" she said. "What does a sister feel seeing her brother lying there dead? Only one person in this courtroom knows the truth," she said, "and he, I hope, will spend the rest of his life wondering was it worth it."

Amber Peck's mother, Glenda Peck, talked about a talented daughter who had won a scholarship to Australia to study animals in pursuit of a veterinarian degree.

"Amber had been an animal lover since she was a child. She cried at the zoo because animals were in cages."

Amber's father, David Peck, spoke emotionally in his daughter's words to Leo in the courtroom: "You are such a coward. You hid in the bushes and waited for me and Johnny to approach you, then came up to me as I was crying and screaming for you to let me live...Though I only had a flesh wound, you came up to me and put the rifle to my head and pulled the trigger to silence me forever...The most important thing for you to know is that you did not silence me and my dreams...They will continue to be heard long and loud. I will not be silenced."

Glenda Peck said she struggled with the life-or-death decision. "I really had a hard time," she said. "I feel like I'm cheating my daughter. But my husband is the one who said she would not have wanted to kill him."

State Attorney Brad King said his office was confident it could obtain a death sentence, but the families wanted a quicker resolution, and he respected their wishes.

"When a family is faced with that dilemma, if I can oblige their wishes...I try to do that," he said. "While we did give up the death penalty, he will be in prison for the rest of his life."

Chief Assistant Public Defender Bill Miller spoke just a little about the defendant's past.

"He had an absolutely horrific life," he said. "No one is making an excuse. It's an enormous offense. He accepted an enormous penalty. Thankfully, it is not the ultimate penalty."

Leo's confession, hard work on the part of his public defenders and a desire on the part of the victims' families for closure led to a plea agreement, which State Attorney Brad King and Judge Pope approved. Leo pled guilty to two counts of first-degree murder and was sentenced to life in prison without any chance of parole. He had avoided the death penalty but would spend his life locked up behind prison walls. The desire of the Parker and Peck families for closure was significant.

The extensive mitigation statement Leo's public defenders had prepared wasn't presented once the death penalty was taken out of consideration. The victims' families chose to use the time in court to talk about their loved ones and to avoid casting the spotlight on Leo Boatman.

"I can't offer an explanation because there is none...I'm sorry," Leo told Circuit Judge Willard Pope and the victims' families.

"He expressed in open court his remorse," Bill Miller added. "He certainly was struck emotionally by the statements of the victims' families."

Leo also spoke to a reporter from the *St. Petersburg Times*. "I had a choice," he said. "I feel like if things were different, I would have been a different person. At the same time, that doesn't excuse anything."

Victor Boatman, Leo's uncle, spoke freely to the press. He said his nephew Leo was dating a stripper as well as a girl who worked at Hooters, where Leo also worked as kitchen help. "On the surface, he has been doing everything right," Vic Boatman said. "He wants to be part of the family again."

His uncle also said that Leo was "an ornery kid, in trouble since he was very young." He admitted that no one in the family visited Leo in his commitment programs except for his grandmother, who died when Leo was fourteen.

After pleading guilty to the murders on July 30, 2007, a few days after his twenty-first birthday, Leo was booked into Cross City Correctional Institute. Having been locked up all of his teenage years without appropriate therapy, Leo was understandably unhappy, angry, and difficult to get along with in prison. He was small for his age. Easy for the guards to harass. Two years later he pled guilty to attempted murder after admitting that he jammed blood pressure medication down the throat of his cell mate and tried to hang him.

According to investigative reports, a corrections officer found Mark "Apple Sauce" Apicella, 34, dangling from the top bunk, struggling to free himself of Boatman's knotted, bedsheet noose. Apicella, who was serving time for theft, organized fraud and cocaine possession, told prison officials that Leo was upset because Apicella got more mail than he did.

Leo told investigators he had not intended to kill Apicella "but sometimes you just get real mad." He insisted that Apicella started the fight. Regardless, Leo received a seven-year sentence for the altercation, and he was moved to the Charlotte Correctional Institution outside of Punta Gorda, Florida.

Leo began there as a "closed population inmate," which is almost like solitary confinement. His behavior improved and he was rising close to being an "open population inmate," meaning he could work on the prison grounds or laundry and mingle with other inmates. He could start to take college classes online and have unlimited library privileges.

Leo told others that he wasn't worried about rape when he got into an open population.

"There is so much consensual sex," he said. "No one has to rape another inmate. It's called 'rocking to sleep,' and inmates trade it for items from the canteen." His main complaint about the Charlotte prison came when they changed the food to basically soy products. "Everything," he said, "whether they call it tuna salad, sloppy joes or chicken, is made of soy. It's disgusting and boring."

In the summer of 2010, Leo was looking forward to more open management when his life changed again.

Ricky Morris, an inmate in closed confinement in another cell at the Charlotte prison, got into a fight with his cell mate, an older, weaker, feeble man the other prisoners called "Pops." Morris nearly gouged an eye out of Pops. Morris was serving life without parole for shooting both of his parents to death in the family home in Florida's Panhandle. He was just a few years older than Leo and was not to be housed with another inmate with a propensity for violence.

After breaking up the fight with Pops in the middle of the night, the guards took Morris out of his cell and moved him into Leo's cell. Prisoners who witnessed the move began chanting angry words directed towards Morris, for beating Pops. Leo clearly wasn't supposed to be housed with Morris, or any inmate like him.

According to Leo, after the guards left and the inmates in adjoining cells settled down, Morris wouldn't quit "talking shit." He bragged about nearly gouging out Pops' eye. Leo tried to fall asleep, but Morris kept laughing and snarling.

Leo said he "got up to pee," and Morris put his arms around him from behind. Leo spun around and threw the first punch. They began fighting. Leo pounded Morris' head with both fists. Morris hit back and began scratching Leo on his head and back. Leo struck Morris hard on his right ear, causing him to fall to his knees and then to the ground in a pool of blood gushing from his ear. Leo banged on the window to call the guard, who finally called for help to open the cell door, remove Leo and get medical help for Morris, unconscious on the cell floor.

Morris was hospitalized and died a month later, never regaining consciousness. His aunt criticized prison guards, saying that Morris should never have been placed with another inmate. She said he was bipolar, delusional and violent. He had shot his parents to death, didn't they know. Once again, she took care of funeral arrangements.

Leo was charged with second-degree murder for the death of Ricky Morris. He was transferred to Florida State Prison in Raiford, Florida. He was housed above the inmates on death row. His privileges were extremely restricted. Visitors were limited. Television rare. He spent most of his time alone in his cell without contact with other inmates or sufficient reading material. He continued to write about the inhumanity of the prison system and complained that prison officials were withholding his mail. His behavior worsened and then improved as he tried to get the severe restrictions lifted.

The State of Florida charged Leo with second-degree murder, contending that he had a "depraved mind" and was motivated to kill Morris by "malice" and "ill will." The state was seeking another life sentence for Leo. Toby Oonk and Don McFarland, experienced public defenders in the felony division in Charlotte County, first tried to get the state to dismiss the case on the basis of mutual combat, self-defense and because of the prison guards' mistake putting two violent convicted murderers in the same cell. The state refused. Leo pled not guilty.

After a number of pre-trials and continuances, a special week was set aside for the jury trial to begin in Charlotte County's criminal justice center on Monday, August 12, 2013.

Chapter 16

Author's Note

Jury trials of defendants charged with murder of another inmate in prison while serving a life without parole sentence are rare. Unless the state is seeking the death penalty, which almost never occurs under this circumstance, the defendant prisoner usually pleads to the charge, or a lesser included charge.

Why would the state waste taxpayer money prosecuting a defendant who will never see the light of day anyway? Aren't public defenders already overworked trying to keep defendants out of prison? Will jurors sympathize with the victim inmate, especially a violent, brutal one?

In Leo Boatman's case he was fortunate, in fact very lucky, to have two public defenders represent him who took his defense very seriously. From the beginning, they worked together closely to examine and challenge every facet of the State's case. They spent a great deal of time with Leo, going over the facts again and again, understanding events from his perspective and preparing him for a four-day trial.

It was an extraordinary experience for me to see Leo in court all four days of the trial and to visit with him afterwards in the Charlotte County Jail. He recognized the long hours, hard work and skilled advocacy of his lawyers. He rose to the occasion and seemed to blossom in a suit and tie, listening to his lawyers rebut the state's evidence with conviction.

Those lawyers, Toby Oonk and Don McFarland, told the jury that Leo Boatman was not "depraved." For the first time in his life, Leo Boatman had a real advocate, in fact two experienced professionals fighting for him.

Those lawyers convinced themselves that Leo was not depraved. The fact that they believed this led Leo to trust in them and to feel better about himself, perhaps for the first time in his life.

No matter the outcome of the trial.

Chapter 17

In Leo's Words—Trial for Another Murder: Day 1
Voir Dire – August 2013

My fingers trembled as I dressed in the Charlotte County Jail that morning. Not because I was nervous about the trial. Hell no, I couldn't wait for it to begin and for it to be over. It was my chance to prove myself innocent, and it had been three years almost to the day since that fight in my prison cell.

My fingers trembled around the maroon and gold tie I somehow had to loop around the blue dress shirt the public defender's office loaned me to wear at trial. They also sent over a darker blue suit, about two sizes too big but pretty sharp. I had never tied a tie before. I wore a clip-on tie for my First Communion. I don't remember wearing one after that. Here I was, 27 years old and tying a tie for the first time. Says something about my life.

Somehow, I got the knot in, figuring that Toby or Don could straighten it out when I met them in the courthouse. I had to do this without a mirror to look in, so naturally it wasn't perfect. I was actually looking forward to seeing their expressions when they saw me dressed in a business suit. Also, I'd asked that my head be shaved as well as the short beard and mustache I'd grown in prison.

I was really impressed with Toby and Don as my lawyers. They met with me every day last week to prepare for the trial. They went over all the witnesses and evidence. They asked me what I thought. We were sort of like a team. I knew they were going to fight hard for me. That doesn't always happen with public defenders. Prisoners make jokes about them not being *real* lawyers, not being prepared or caving in too easily. Not Toby and Don. They'd already won some key points.

First was the matter of court security. The state wanted four armed deputy sheriffs in uniforms surrounding me throughout the trial. Ridiculous, Toby told the judge. It would make me look like a terrorist. I remembered the first pre-trial hearing when three deputies stood next to me wearing black face masks along with their uniforms and guns. I guess they had heard that I had spit blood at the guards in the juvenile prison. That was years ago. I wasn't about to pull that stunt at this trial. Anyway, Toby convinced the judge to instruct two of the guards to wear street clothes and sit behind me in the gallery. They would look like spectators, or maybe like family or friends. The two in uniforms, wearing guns, could stand behind me, but they would blend into the background. Jurors were used to seeing armed guards in court, the state argued.

Then, Toby and Don won a key ruling before the trial began. The state could not tell the jury that I was convicted of murdering two college students or that I was serving a life without parole sentence. Of course it cut both ways. My lawyers couldn't tell the jury that Ricky Morris had shot to death both his parents. All the jury would know was that Morris and I were inmates at Charlotte Correctional Institution when the incident happened. I figured that was really good for me. If the jury knew I was serving a life sentence, they might say, "What the hell," and just convict me again.

Even Deputy Fox had a little smile on his face when he saw me in my fancy blue suit and tie. As ordered, two of the deputies were wearing street clothes, polo shirts and jeans. Their guns were well hidden. All four escorted me from the jail to the van and we drove to the courthouse, where I met my lawyers and took a seat between them at the defense table. The deputies sat or stood as instructed.

The courtroom was very modern with grey or white walls and a big window behind where I sat overlooking the Peace River. The wall behind the judge was made up of wood paneling, set in large squares. A gold and bronze circle, the official seal of the Great State of Florida, hung in the middle of the paneling behind the raised bench where Judge Amy Hawthorne sat. She had long straight blonde hair, parted in the middle, and large eyeglasses with clear frames. She looked on the young side for a circuit judge. The jury box was to her right, with twelve comfortable black chairs. They wouldn't be empty for long, I thought, wondering what type of person would occupy them. It better be someone who liked air conditioning, as it was cold in the courtroom.

After an hour of hearing jury excuses—doctor's appointments, sick relatives, important business to attend to—Judge Hawthorne ordered the remaining jurors from the jury pool to be seated to begin the voir dire. She already struck me as a pretty tough judge. She didn't excuse any jurors who said they were hard of hearing. Rather, she had court personnel bring them a device that made everything sound louder.

"Welcome to the Criminal Justice Center," Judge Hawthorne addressed the jury panel, which seemed to me to be mostly middle-aged women. "We are here for the trial of the case of the State of Florida versus Leo Lansing Boatman. We will make every effort to make you comfortable and to be efficient if you are chosen for this jury. We anticipate the trial will take five days. We will work from 9 a.m. to 5 p.m., with breaks in the morning and afternoon and an hour for lunch."

She instructed the lawyers to introduce themselves and me to the jury and to read the list of witnesses expected to be called by either side.

"Does anyone know any of the lawyers, Mr. Boatman or anyone expected to be a witness in the case?" No one raised a hand, so she asked the lead state attorney, Scott Patterson, to begin the voir dire.

Scott Patterson, the lead state attorney, square-jawed and with light brown hair styled somewhere between a short Mohawk and a long crew cut, began with a bang—the state's charge against me.

"The State of Florida has charged the defendant, Leo Boatman, with second-degree murder, alleging that on August 18, 2010, the defendant, Leo Boatman, while in a depraved state of mind, murdered Ricky Morris, who died September 19, 2010. Does anyone here know anything about the case?"

No one raised their hand. Was I imagining it, or did Patterson draw out the word "depraaaaaved," so the jury wouldn't miss it? I had looked up the word in a dictionary. It meant perverted, immoral or corrupted.

Patterson continued by asking the questions my lawyers said would be asked by prosecutors:

"Have any of you been victims of a crime?" "Have any of you been charged with a crime?" "Had friends or relatives charged with a crime?"

Every time a juror raised a hand, Patterson asked for details and took notes. It seemed to me more people had been charged with some kind of crime, or knew someone who had, than had been victims of crime themselves.

"Law enforcement officers will testify in this case," he said. "Do any of you have a bias towards law enforcement? Have friends or relatives who have been police officers or prison guards?"

This drew a lot of comments from the jury, a few saying they "held police officers in admiration," or "would respect what law enforcement said." One middle-aged lady who had an answer for every question asked told Patterson, "I may have an underlying bias towards police officers, but I feel I can be fair." Previously, she described a "home invasion" in which she was the victim, she and her dog "scared to death."

"If I'm chosen," she said, "I pride myself on my honesty so I will be objective."

"She's history," Toby whispered to me. "She wants so badly to be a juror. She cares too much about this case."

When Patterson continued to focus on law enforcement, Judge Hawthorne interrupted him.

"Every witness is on equal footing," she told the jury panel. "Law enforcement officers are not to be given any greater weight in their testimony," she said, moving Patterson off the topic.

"Does everyone believe that crimes in prison should be prosecuted, not just resolved by the prisons?" Patterson asked the jury panel. Most nodded their heads in agreement.

"Do we care what happens between two inmates or should crimes be resolved within the prison walls?" Patterson got a little push back on this, as one male juror asked, "What about schools? They're supposed to solve stuff in the schools, aren't they?"

Patterson was good. He was ready for this. "But what if it's a very serious crime? Shouldn't we bring it to court? Don't we have a responsibility to take care of inmates in prison? To protect them from crimes? Do we say, he was just a prisoner, so it's a waste of court time?"

The jury was nodding with him. They bought his line. I'm no lawyer, obviously, but I could see what he was doing. Priming the jury to feel sorry for Morris, and to convict me.

Patterson sat down and Don McFarland stood up to begin the voir dire for the defense. Don is tall, grey haired and distinguished looking with a big Irish smile. The first thing he said made me feel ten feet tall and happier than I'd been in a long time.

"Welcome, ladies and gentlemen. My colleague, Toby Oonk, and I are proud to be representing our client, Leo Boatman." He gestured toward me and thirty or so people turned their eyes on me. I smiled slightly and nodded my head.

"Who here believes that they are completely impartial and unbiased?" Don asked. They looked confused, like it was a trick question. No one raised a hand.

"That's right," Don continued. "We all have biases and prejudices. What we want you to do in the courtroom is put those aside. To become unbiased jurors in this case. To rely on the evidence presented in this courtroom."

Don then moved closer to the defense table. "When you walk into the courtroom and see defense counsel at the table, and a guy who's introduced as the defendant, what thoughts do you have about him? Do you think he's just a guy, or do you think he must be guilty because he's sitting there?"

This got a few laughs from the panel, and one woman raised her hand with a question for Don.

"Could you tell us again who the defendant is?" she asked.

Don pointed to me, I stood up again and the lady said, "Oh, I thought he was your law clerk or something." That brought more laughter.

"When someone is charged with a crime, it doesn't mean they are guilty, does it?" Don continued. Heads were nodding, no. "But it doesn't mean they are not guilty either." The jury panel was hanging on his every word. "Because they are *presumed* innocent. It's not a level playing field. The accused has a *presumption* that he's innocent. Leo Boatman has the advantage. He's *presumed* to be innocent, and the state has the burden of proving to you that he's guilty *beyond a reasonable doubt.*"

"Do you all agree to give Leo Boatman that presumption that the law grants to him? To hold the state to that burden, to rebut the presumption?"

They shook their heads in agreement.

"You know," he said, "it is human nature when we are driving and see another motorist pulled over by the police on the side of the road, to wonder what they did. Very seldom do we ask ourselves what they *didn't* do."

"But this is a criminal courtroom, not a public street." He then posed a question. "Now, when you look at a defendant at a defense table and the first thing you wonder is what he did to get there, ask yourself what he *didn't* do. Because in this courtroom, under the law of the land, this defendant, Leo Boatman, is *presumed* innocent."

"Damn, he is good," I said to myself as Don took his seat next to me.

Chapter 18

Trial for Another Murder: Day 2

Opening Statements and Prison Guard Crosby

While I knotted my tie, a pinstriped one this time, and pulled the loose jacket over my shoulders, I had a weird sensation that I was normal, like everyone else in town, going off to work. I hadn't ever felt like that. It was a fantasy that felt good and one I didn't want to disappear. I even smiled and joked around with Deputy Fox and the other guards who escorted me to my seat at the defense table. We'd picked a jury, and I was expecting them to be seated momentarily and for opening statements to begin.

Then, the shit hit the fan, so to speak.

Before excusing the jury last evening, Judge Hawthorne had read to them a long warning about what they weren't supposed to do. No talking about the case with friends, relatives or each other. No watching any TV news about the case or reading any newspaper articles about it. No researching anything related to the case on the internet. No texting, tweeting or skyping to others about the case. She really covered all the bases and looked sternly at the six jurors and four alternate jurors, asking them if they understood. They all nodded or answered "yes."

So you can understand why she was upset when someone told her that two of the jurors had read that morning's *Charlotte*

Sun newspaper. The front page headline read: "Convicted Killer on Trial" and underneath that, "Prison inmate accused of beating cell mate to death." Out of the presence of the jury, Assistant State Attorney Patterson argued that the newspaper article was very short and mostly factual. Toby was incensed, and quickly pointed out to the judge the part of the article that said, "Court records show Boatman allegedly killed his CCI cell mate, Ricky Morris, 28, by 'punching, kicking, stomping and beating the victim and repeatedly smashing the victim's face onto a cement floor.'" In case that wasn't enough, Toby read to the judge the part that said I had pled guilty in July 2007 to killing with an AK-47 assault rifle two college students who were camping in the Ocala National Forest.

It wasn't a hard decision for Judge Hawthorne. She said that's why we have alternate jurors. Then she had those two jurors brought into the courtroom and told them they were excused from further jury service. She didn't act angry in front of them. It seemed like she was just about thanking them for blabbing to someone about what they had read. Next, she told the first two alternate jurors that they were no longer alternates but actual members of the jury. Of course, she instructed them all again on what they were not supposed to do, read or watch on television.

The jury was pretty evenly divided, men and women; old, middle aged and young; minorities and whites. I wouldn't call it a "jury of my peers," like they say in all the murder mysteries I've read, but then who are my peers now anyway? Prison inmates? Other lifers? Anyway, the jury settled down and looked awake when Patterson gave his opening statement.

I was kind of surprised. I expected him to get dramatic, point me out again as a depraved man. Instead, he took just seven minutes to lay out a factual case, going through the events in sequence, from Morris's placement in my cell to the beating and eventual death. He did say that the victim, Morris, "was not a saint." Well, I guess not, I think to myself.

After all, he murdered both his parents. But the jury doesn't know that, just like they don't know why I was convicted and ended up in that cell.

Toby was brilliant in his opening for the defense. He and Don made great partners as they looked completely different. Don was tall and fair haired and made you want to like him. Toby was short with dark hair and angular features and made you want to listen to him so you didn't miss a trick. They couldn't be working as public defenders for the money. They must have really believed in what they were doing as they were pretty damn good lawyers and could have been making big bucks elsewhere.

Anyway, Toby started by describing prison life. "Prison is its own world. It's encircled by a chain link fence and heavy barbed wire. In there, unable to leave, prisoners build relationships or destroy them." He stretched his arms out like he was flying. "In eight-foot by eight-foot cells—the width of my arms—violence, brutality and tough guys live together."

Toby told the jury that they would hear from Pops, the old guy that Morris beat up, almost gouging out his eye, before Morris was moved into my cell. Pops would make a good witness, I thought. His real name was Danny Willis. He was sixty-seven years old and had been in prison over thirty years for an armed robbery he committed back in 1974. He looked like someone's grandfather and was very calm.

Finally, Toby warned the jury to keep an open mind, listen to all the evidence and think about the lack of evidence. How little the state had to meet their burden of proving I was guilty beyond a reasonable doubt.

The state's first witness was Crosby, the guard who patrolled the quad the night of the fight. I almost lost my cool when he swore to tell the truth, because he lied in his investigation, he lied in his report, and I was damn sure he would lie again in court. More than any other person involved in this case, he was responsible for me being here. He changed his story from breaking up a fight to saying I was responsible for Morris's death.

Then a funny thing happened. Don told me he had never seen it happen before in court. Just when Crosby was describing how many times he made his rounds, looking in my cell, finding everything fine and Morris and me "getting along well," and then looking in three hours later to find Morris on the ground and me "covered in blood," a juror, the older Black man in the back, raised his hand. When the judge asked him if he needed a break or something, he said, "No, I just want to point out that the witness contradicted himself. He said something different a little while ago."

First there was silence. Then a few people laughed. Crosby turned red. The judge hid a little smile and told the juror that he could take that into consideration, but he couldn't interrupt the testimony. Don and Toby looked down, trying to hide their smiles. Good, I thought. No one deserved to be called a liar more than Crosby.

I looked behind me into the audience to see if there was a reaction. What I saw made me feel really happy and grateful. My Uncle Vic, or maybe he was my brother Vic since my grandmother adopted me, or maybe he was still my Uncle Vic because she gave me back to the state—anyway, Vic was here in the courtroom. Somehow, he made the two-hour drive from Pinellas County and was here to offer support. We smiled at each other.

On cross exam, Toby pointed out more inconsistencies in Crosby's testimony and incident report. On re-direct, Crosby said what he saw was "more like a beating than a fight." But on re-cross, Toby got him to admit that the tiny window in the cell made it impossible to see Morris on the floor, and that it took him awhile to gather other guards to be able to enter my cell. I just hoped the other jurors thought like the old guy and recognized Crosby for what he was: a liar who was covering his ass.

One thing that made this case different from others was the amount of surveillance tapes available for the jury to see. I'd seen them all in preparing for this trial with Toby and Don. My favorite tape was the first one that we'd see that day. It showed two guards walking Morris from the cell where he brutally beat up Pops down the corridor to my cell. Pops was a pretty popular inmate, so when word got out that Morris attacked him, you could hear the other inmates banging their doors and yelling as Morris and the guards passed. On the tape, you could see that Morris was carrying two laundry bags in his hands, which were handcuffed behind him, and he sure didn't look hurt at all. Then, as he got to my cell, he turned to the right and snarled and lunged at the inmate in that cell, who was cussing him out. I mean it. This was a vicious guy. Even surrounded by guards and handcuffed, he lunged, bared his teeth and snapped and growled at another inmate. He looked like an animal. Worse than an animal, in fact, unless it's a dog with rabies.

We rested for the day. I hoped tonight the jurors would have visions of Ricky Morris snarling at them.

Chapter 19

Trial for Another Murder:
Day 3
The State and Defense Rest

Today is jam-packed with witnesses for the state, photographs and surveillance films. I can see that the jury is really paying attention when the films are shown. Each juror has a small TV screen fixed to their chair to view the films. I look at the big screen in the courtroom. I guess that is the advantage of prison-based crimes: you have films of a lot of what happened.

The first films are sort of sickening. They show the guards entering my cell and finding Morris unconscious on the ground, lying in a lot of blood. The cameraman pans the tiny cell, filming the bunk beds—really cots, not beds—the stainless steel toilet and sink and the bench opposite the cell door. Then some medical people from the infirmary arrive and they drag Morris by his feet to a place where they put him on a stretcher. They put an oxygen mask and blood pressure cuff on him. You can see the tattoos on his stomach, his close-cropped brown hair and the bloodied chin, eye and ear. His chest is heaving in the beginning, but by the time they take him out on the stretcher, he is breathing easier. Someone wipes the blood off his face. He is taken to the infirmary where an EKG is hooked up and a tube is put in his mouth to connect to portable oxygen. Leg restraints are put on his feet, "just in case." Morris is then transferred by the Charlotte County emergency technicians to the local hospital.

The next video is introduced by another prison guard,

James Bullvack. It shows a guard escorting me from the cell after the fight. Contrary to Crosby's testimony, there is no blood on my white T-shirt, my white boxer shorts or my arms, feet or legs. If I'd pounded Morris's head on the cement floor, as Crosby said, wouldn't there be blood all over me? The film goes on to show me taken to the infirmary, where my blood pressure is taken. I'm given fresh clothes and taken to the shower.

Then, unbelievably, three grainy black and white photographs of me behind the bars of a cell were introduced to show that I had no injuries in the fight. The photos were unclear, blurred and not at all as professional as an investigation would warrant. They were taken through steel mesh. I was wearing my T-shirt the entire time. Toby made a huge point that no one had asked me to take off my shirt to look for evidence of injuries. They just took these awful pictures and then claimed I wasn't injured, ignoring the scratches on my back and the back of my head. Toby really trashed these photographs as being anything but helpful in an investigation. I thought the jury got his point.

On cross exam, Toby got some good testimony about how cooperative I was, coming to the cell window to get the guard's attention, not delaying entry into my cell, walking calmly and slowly to the infirmary and shower. He also got an admission that Ricky Morris should not have been placed in my cell had the guards known all the facts that night.

Objections were made by both sides to some of the evidence. It wasn't as exciting as on TV or in a novel. The lawyers didn't really state their grounds. As soon as they said "objection," Judge Hawthorne called them up to the side of her bench, away from the jury, along with the court reporter. When everyone was situated, the bailiff turned a machine on that sent a buzzing sound through the courtroom so no one could hear what was said anyway. It was annoying but I guess it was necessary to keep the jury from hearing arguments.

The next witness, Lee Dewey, a crime scene investigator from the Florida Department of Law Enforcement, turned out to help us more than he hurt us. Although he testified to the large amount of blood spatters in the cell, he admitted on cross that if Morris shook his head on account of the blow to the ear, it could cause significant blood spatters. He also said the bloody footprints on the floor and the bloody handprints on the cot were not necessarily mine. He said that "blood smearing" could have come from the nurses walking around the cell to administer initial first aid, or from Morris being dragged out of the cell to be placed on a stretcher. Luminol spray would have detected footprints made by others, and it wasn't used, he said.

The doctors testified next. A forensic pathologist and the hospital's chief of staff, a trauma specialist. Basically they agreed that Morris suffered a severe head injury that caused him to become unconscious for a month, leading to his death from pneumonia, as he couldn't clear fluid from his lungs. That was it in a nutshell, but as usual in court it takes hours to make that point.

The doctors showed slides that showed bleeding in the brain area. They pointed to areas of swelling and pressure to the side of the skull. Although they agreed that there was no evidence of fractures to the skull, they still testified that the head injuries Morris sustained could have come from a "pounding" on the cement floor. They stuck to their simple cause of death: respiratory failure. If Morris hadn't had the brain injury, he wouldn't have contracted the pneumonia which caused the respiratory failure and death. It seemed pretty straightforward to me, and I didn't think the jury was confused. We couldn't win these witnesses over, I thought.

Toby did the best he could do in cross exam. He got one doctor to identify an old injury to Morris's brain. The other doctor admitted that there were many kinds of pneumonia, not all causing respiratory failure. She identified a fracture to Morris's right hand, which she called a "boxer's fracture" caused by balling the fist for a fistfight. Helpful to us was testimony that the left lung was almost twice the size of the right lung, meaning the pneumonia could have developed before the head injury. Also, in the autopsy there was no evidence of injury to internal organs. Best of all, one of the doctors let slip that Morris was bi-polar, schizophrenic and manic depressive, according to family members. But, upon redirect by the state, the medical testimony was consistent that the major injuries caused by trauma to the head led to complications that caused death. The final nail in the coffin was the clear testimony that the injuries couldn't be caused from falling off a bed or slipping to the floor. Not good for us.

So I wasn't feeling happy after the doctors' testimony. I had read their depositions. They certainly sounded more positive and surer of themselves in person.

During the afternoon break, Toby, Don and I slip into a strategy session. This is an important moment in the trial. One of the things I've regretted every day since I was appointed legal counsel is the very stupid statement I made to prison officials investigating the incident a day or two after it happened.

I'd been led to believe that the guard Crosby and others were satisfied that the fight was either mutual combat or self-defense on my part. So, when I was asked to give a formal statement of what happened, other things went through my head. I was still angry that they had placed Ricky Morris in my cell, the snarling beast. I was in a bad mood when I gave the statement and I was also thinking I had to sound tough, as word gets around and I didn't want to be attacked by other inmates. I was still small, about 5'8" and 145 pounds. Finally, I was being somewhat manipulative, thinking I might get something in return for the right words in my statement.

So I basically told the investigators something like: "I hope the fucker dies. He shouldn't have beaten up an old man. He got what he deserved. He never stood a chance with me. If you guys aren't going to work with me, like giving me more privileges, something to do, so that I have something to lose if I act up, then this is what I'll do." Can you imagine how dumb of me that was? So, as soon as the officials got that statement, they revised their investigation to support a charge of murder in the second degree, the result of a "depraved" mind and "ill will" to the victim. I dug my own grave.

Toby and Don had tried hard in pre-trial motions to keep the jury from hearing that statement, but it was clear that the judge was going to let the prosecutors introduce it into evidence. "It's the one thing that supports a charge of second-degree murder," Toby told me. "You can explain it away as prison bravado or tough talk, but the jury isn't going to feel sympathy for you if they hear it."

So, in this strategy session, Toby told Don and me of his hunch. "I have a hunch," he said, "that the prosecution has placed so much importance on your statement that they want it to be the last piece of evidence the jury hears. The only way they can do that is to rest their case in chief now, let us put on our case, and in the rebuttal they are entitled to bring their witnesses in to talk about your statement and get it into evidence."

"That would be very effective," Don said. I agreed. That stupid statement could mean another murder conviction and another life sentence.

"So," Toby continued. "I have a hunch that the prosecutors are so confident that we will put on a case, such as your self-defense claim, Pops' testimony as to the viciousness of Ricky Morris, etc., that they are ready to rest their case and let us begin the defense. When we are through, they will march in their rebuttal witnesses with your statement, probably photographed for the jurors to read on their TVs."

Don smiled wide. He knew what Toby had in mind.

"Therefore, if we rest our case after they rest theirs, in other words put nothing on by way of a defense, not Leo, not

Pops, there is nothing to rebut, and the testimony is over. On to closing arguments, jury instructions and a verdict."

Now it took a little while for me to get a handle on this. I had been prepared to testify. I wanted to tell the jury how Morris talked shit, then grabbed me around the waist. Especially since the jury had seen the film of Morris snarling and lunging himself at the other prisoner, I thought they could see that I had a right and a need to defend myself. At the very least, they might find mutual combat and acquit. But Toby was right. That dumb statement was the worst evidence against me. Any way to keep it from the jury appealed to me.

"Do you understand, Leo?" Don asked. "If you agree with what Toby suggests, the testimony ends when the state rests and the defense rests. You won't get the chance to testify. I think it's a great strategy and that the prosecutors have made a grave mistake to rely on rebuttal testimony to get that statement in. But I want to make sure you understand what you're giving up. We can't argue self-defense or mutual combat in closing. We just have to argue a lack of evidence on the part of the state. Of course, the state won't have your careless statement to argue that you are a depraved mind."

"I get it," I said. "I think it's a good trade off."

"Okay," Toby said, heading back to the courtroom. "Let's see what the state does."

The jury was seated after we had taken our seats at the defense table. For the first time, it occurred to me to wonder if the jury knew that I was in prison now. They'd heard of an incident at Charlotte Correctional Institution three years ago, but Don had carefully stated in his voir dire that it was where I was "once housed." They didn't know about the murders of the college kids. And I was wearing this nice blue suit. Anyway, I was anxious to see what the state would do next.

"The State of Florida rests its case, your honor," Patterson said, standing before Judge Hawthorne. "What says the defense?" she said, looking at our table.

"The defense has a motion to make," Toby said. Judge Hawthorne asked deputies to take the jury from the room. Toby then made the standard defense motion for judgment of dismissal following the state's case. A routine motion and usually denied. I thought it was a pretty good motion.

"Your honor," Toby began, "this is a second-degree murder charge. Yes, the victim is dead, the first element of the crime. But the state has put on no evidence, direct or indirect, that it was caused by the defendant or why the act occurred. There are no statements from Mr. Boatman, no evidence of a relationship between the victim and defendant, no evidence of a depraved mind, ill will or intent. An impulsive overreaction is not enough. There must be evidence of a more serious state of mind than for manslaughter. There must be evidence of animosity between the victim and the defendant. Simply put, there isn't any, your honor. The state's own witness, the guard, Crosby, said the two men were getting along famously."

Judge Hawthorne looked to Patterson for his response. Patterson looked agitated and seemed worried that the judge would grant the motion.

"They were getting along at first sight, your honor," Patterson began. "But within two and a half hours, with only two men in a locked cell, the Defendant was observed bashing the victim's head onto the concrete floor, repeatedly, while the victim was unconscious. That in itself is evidence of a depraved state of mind."

"The motion is denied at this time," Judge Hawthorne ruled. Then she turned to the defense table.

"I'm going to bring the jury in so the defense can begin its case this afternoon," she said.

Toby stood again. "Your honor," he said. "The defense also rests."

Chapter 20

Trial for Another Murder: Day 4

Giving up the Right to Testify

It was clear to me now, as I put on a blue and white polka dot tie and buttoned the sleeves of my blue dress shirt, that the trial would end today. I was definitely nervous. My stomach was upset.

Yesterday afternoon had been pretty dramatic.

When Toby announced that the defense rested its case, before putting on any witnesses or evidence, the prosecutors were stunned. They looked at each other first in surprise and then dismay. They had witnesses outside the courtroom ready to rebut anything I said on the stand, and they had my written statement to boot. Now it was over. The statement wouldn't come into evidence. They were pissed.

The judge looked surprised too, then she smiled a little. That's about the most emotion she would show during the entire trial.

"Mr. Boatman," she said to me. "If you are not going to testify, by law I have to ask you some questions."

I stood up next to the defense table.

"Do you understand you have the absolute right to testify on your own behalf?"

"I do," I said.

"Do you understand that you are waiving that right to testify on your own behalf?"

"I do," I said.

"Have you discussed this matter with your attorneys, Mr. Boatman?" she said.

"I have, your honor," I replied.

"Are you all in agreement that you wish not to testify?"

"Yes," I said.

"Very well," she said. "That concludes the testimony then. We can recess for tonight. The attorneys and I will use this extra time to review the jury instructions. I will instruct the jury to return at nine a.m. tomorrow morning for the closing arguments."

Toby and Don had been whispering to each other while I was answering the judge's questions. Now Toby rose to address the court.

"Your honor," he said. "Before I call off our witnesses, I want to make sure the state isn't going to raise any motions or try to do anything to re-open their case. I know the law wouldn't allow it, as there is no newly-discovered evidence, but I want to make sure today that they don't pull something tomorrow. So, can we tell our witnesses to go home, that they won't be needed?"

Judge Hawthorne smiled a bit again. "Counsel, you know I can't advise you on this matter. You have to do what you think is best. You have to decide how to prepare." She turned to the prosecution table.

"Mr. Patterson, your response?"

"Judge, we'll consider all our options this evening," he said.

Toby raised his voice, pointing at the prosecutor. "Make them do it now, Judge. If they are going to ask the court for some relief, make them do it now," he demanded.

"Mr. Oonk," she said, still pleasant. "I'm not going to make either side play their hand earlier than the law allows. Bailiff, bring the jury in so I can advise them that they can go home for the evening. Counsel, once they leave, I will see you in my chambers to go over the jury instructions."

Once the jury left, I had a few minutes to talk to Toby and

Don before I was taken back to the jail.

"What was that about?" I asked.

Don spoke first. "Toby's concerned that the state might move to re-open the case on some theory of surprise or something. The law shouldn't allow it. It was their strategy to wait until rebuttal to get your statement in. They blew it. But you can never be certain how the judge will rule if they find any case law to support a motion to re-open."

"So we really won't know until tomorrow morning?" I asked.

"True," Don said. "But don't let it keep you awake. I saw the judge suppress a big grin when Toby said we rested our case. She knows exactly what's going on. She's fully aware that your statement has been a hot topic since proceedings began. Remember how hard we tried to get her to keep it out of evidence, but we really didn't have grounds to do so? The judge was a darn good public defender before she took the bench. There's no way she's going to allow the state to re-open the case. She knows they just made a big mistake."

"Get a good night's sleep. It might be a long day tomorrow," Toby said as the guards took me from the courtroom and the two lawyers headed for Judge Hawthorne's chambers. I nodded at Uncle Vic, who rose in the gallery and smiled at me. I wished he could visit with me before I was taken back to the jail, but it couldn't happen.

Chapter 21

Trial for Another Murder: Day 5
Closings

So here we were again, the morning of the last day of the trial, waiting for the state to make its move.

"Are there any motions to be made by either side?" Judge Hawthorne asked the lawyers before the jury was brought into the courtroom.

We all looked at the prosecutors. Patterson stood up.

"No, your honor," he said.

Toby smiled, also standing. "No, your honor," he said.

Whew, I thought. We dodged a bullet.

"Then let's bring the jury in and begin the closing arguments," she motioned to the bailiff.

When the jurors had taken their seats, Judge Hawthorne welcomed them back.

"The lawyers are now going to present their closing arguments. Again, what they say is not evidence, but their arguments about the evidence. If your recollection of the evidence differs from theirs, you should feel free to rely on your memory. The state will make the first closing argument, then the defense and then the state will have a brief rebuttal argument.

"Mr. Patterson," she said. "You may proceed."

I thought it was definitely unfair that the state got the first and last argument, especially because we hadn't put on a defense case. Toby told me the law was changed that way about seven years ago. Really unfair, I thought. Two bites of the apple.

"Ladies and gentlemen of the jury," he began, holding up a picture of the small window to my cell. "This is a window to a murder. And this defendant," he said, walking toward me and pointing at me, "this depraved defendant, committed this murder." Patterson's tone of voice couldn't have been more hateful, more scornful.

"And how did he do it?" he asked. "Like this," he said as he picked a rag doll off the podium, knelt and began smashing the doll's head to the floor. "He slammed the victim's head five or six times onto the cement floor of the cell. The guard saw the defendant wash blood off his hands, then walk over and slam the head of the victim, who was unconscious, again and again.

"This wasn't a fight. It was a beating. A beating, Doctor Hutchins testified, that caused a severe, life-threatening injury to the victim's head."

He got up, his face flushed. "Ladies and gentlemen, it is as it seems. Two men entered the cell. One man is left alive. One man left standing. That defendant," he said again pointing at me. "The murderer."

Patterson put the doll back on the podium and switched subjects.

"Let's talk about causation," he said. "There was a beating. That put the victim in a coma. That placed him on a ventilator. That led to where he couldn't close his airways. Fluid built up, infection set in, pneumonia caused his death. But for the beating, no pneumonia and no death.

"Let's look at the beating," he said, showing the jury a photograph of Morris's face. "Left eye, right eye, bloody. Left ear, almost ripped entirely off. As Dr. Hutchins testified, it is inconceivable that one blow to the head could have caused all these injuries."

He got the doll again, holding it up to the jury.

"What happened to Ricky Morris is similar to shaken baby syndrome. His head was pounded repeatedly on a cement floor. The brain moves back and forth, hitting the inside of the skull each time. Bruising and swelling occurred, according to the doctors, causing a concussion and unconsciousness. Murder, pure and simple.

"Now that we know it is murder, was it justified, as the jury instructions Judge Hawthorne will read to you and ask you to consider.

"It wasn't justified. There's no evidence of that. Ricky Morris didn't do anything. He didn't provoke this beating. It wasn't an accident. It wasn't mutual combat. There's no evidence of a mutual fight.

"Was it second degree murder? Was it the act of a *depraved* mind? A *cruel* person? I ask you, what can be more cruel than tearing an ear three quarters off? Clearly it was murder.

"The state has proven the elements of second-degree murder beyond a reasonable doubt. First, the victim is dead. Second, the death was caused by the criminal act of the defendant, Leo Boatman. Third, the act was imminently dangerous, demonstrating a *depraved* mind, ill will, hatred and spite.

"The whole dorm was angry at Ricky Morris that night for fighting with an older inmate. But only Leo Boatman," he said pointing at me again, "only Leo Boatman is the reason Ricky Morris is dead. One jail cell. Two men. One left alive.

"Leo Boatman washed the blood off his hands that night. But he can't wash off his responsibility for Ricky Martin's death. It's murder, pure and simple."

As Patterson took his seat, I watched the jury. They didn't fidget or move around. Did they buy Patterson's argument? Maybe I was thinking too much like a lawyer now, but I didn't think it was that great a closing argument. I thought it was hokey when he got down on the ground, smashing the rag doll to the floor. And what's with the shaken baby syndrome? That doesn't have anything to do with this case. It's holding a baby and shaking its head back and forth, causing injury. Not smashing a head on a concrete floor, which is what I didn't do, but what the state claims I did. If I had, wouldn't I have fractured his skull? The doctors said there were no skull fractures. I hope that is brought out in our closing.

Don McFarland began our one and only closing argument. As he moved into position, Toby projected to the jurors the video clip of Ricky Morris snarling and lunging at a cell mate, just before entering my cell.

"For centuries," Don said, "people believed the sun revolved around the earth. It made sense. The sun rises in the east and sets in the west. We on earth don't feel like we are revolving. It is simple, so it must be true.

"That's their case, ladies and gentlemen of the jury. It is simple. Two men in a cell. One dead. That equals murder. Simple.

"But it is not so simple, not when you look at the evidence."

He began with the prison guard, Crosby.

"He was a trainee. He transported Ricky Morris from the cell downstairs to Boatman's cell because Morris's behavior was so bad he couldn't stay down there. Watch Morris, as he lunges at another prisoner, after just getting through beating another inmate. He lunges like a junkyard dog. He is anything but calm and quiet. And Mr. Crosby was anything but truthful.

"Crosby claims he made nine passes in the corridor, looking into darkened cells. Well, he couldn't have seen into a darkened cell with just a flashlight. Then Crosby says he discovered Boatman standing at the door. No reaction. This makes no sense.

"What makes sense is that he was summoned by Boatman. Boatman was at his window, trying to get help from a guard. That's what makes sense.

"Crosby says that Leo Boatman was covered in blood. But we see the film of Boatman being taken down to the shower, before changing clothes. Where is the blood? These are good photographs. He's wearing a white T-shirt and shorts. Where is the blood?

"Crosby says he forgot to record it. He's lying, ladies and gentlemen. That alone creates reasonable doubt. There is no blood on Boatman, no blood on his hands or clothes, even though the cell is a bloody mess where Morris was lying, bleeding from the ear.

"The prison has surveillance cameras all over the place, including in the shower. Where are the pictures of Boatman washing the blood off himself in the shower? And how did he wash the blood off his clothes? There are no faint blood stains. Nothing on his white clothes.

"Now look at the testimony of the prison official who investigated the case. Look on your TV screens at the pictures this *investigator* took. Black and white films from some crummy camera. Blurred. Taken while Boatman is behind steel mesh, with his clothes on. No effort to take pictures of the scratches on his back and the back of his head.

"And this investigator says he took the bloody clothes for evidence. Well, where are they? No clothes were produced in the state's case. That's because there are no bloody clothes. There's not even a photo of bloody clothes.

"It is clear that no effort was made to find out what happened in that cell. We know Morris was a violent man. He had a boxer's fracture to his hand. The kind you get from a hard punch.

"Morris had just beaten up on old man, and now, as the picture on your screen shows, he lunges at another inmate. He pounded an old guy, and he lunges and snarls, out of control still, at someone else.

"It's the state's burden in this case," McFarland reminds the jury. "It's up to the state to tell you what happened in that cell, and they didn't.

"Dewey, the crime scene investigator, doesn't back up Crosby. He admits they didn't use Luminol to find smeared blood, footprints, fingerprints. Crosby, a week after, he recalls, finds an opportunity to write the incident report.

"Prison is an unpleasant place. That night, the night Ricky Morris beat up an old man, it was worse than unpleasant. The inmates were screaming and yelling at Morris. They were falling onto steel bunks, beating on the floor. You can hear them in the films.

"Now here is a fact. We *know* Ricky Morris was in a fight that night because that is why he was removed and placed in another cell.

"But there is no evidence of who made that decision. The amount of blood on the floor of the cell is not unusual for a facial injury. Single blunt trauma could have occurred. A fall. It's not up to Mr. Boatman to explain what happened. In this country, it's up to the government. And if you are left with reasonable doubt—after all, there were no skull fractures—then you must acquit.

"To sustain a charge of second-degree murder, there must be first a criminal act of the defendant. Who witnessed this? Crosby? He's not truthful.

"Where is the depraved mind? Leo could have blocked his cell, kept the medics away from Morris. That is a depraved mind. But that didn't happen. We don't know *what* happened.

"Where is the hatred, spite, evil intent? There is no evidence to suggest any of it. Evidence is what you need to make your decision. The defendant was cooperative at all times. Where is the evidence of a depraved mind?

"Judge Hawthorne will instruct you again about reasonable doubt. She will tell you that even if you form an abiding conviction of guilt, if that conviction waivers and vacillates, then the state has not proved the charge beyond every reasonable doubt, and you must find the defendant not guilty. Your doubt must be reasonable, but you can find reasonable doubt by a conflict in the evidence or a lack of evidence.

"Was this a real investigation, a valid investigation? No. It was circling the wagons and blaming Boatman.

"The state promised you a case, but they brought you the sun revolving around the earth. They brought you the *appearance* of a case. Two men in a cell. One man left. Murder. This is not a case. Not in this country.

"You need *evidence* to convict someone in this country. We make the state bring evidence. Here there is nothing but Crosby's testimony. Nothing else.

"Society is measured by how it treats the weakest members. Prisoners have no power. They don't control their lives. They are easy scapegoats for liars and incompetents to hide behind."

Now Don raises his voice.

"Leo Boatman didn't commit murder. There is no evidence of a depraved mind. No bloody clothes. You've seen Leo Boatman in whites walking out of his cell. You've seen Ricky Morris lunging at another prisoner's cell. Consider what you've seen. Leo Boatman is not a murderer."

Patterson looked irritated and rushed when he returned to address the jury.

"Yes," he said. "Ricky Morris had a very bad day. He was murdered.

"Find him guilty," he begged them, pointing again at me.

He picked the doll up again and knelt down. "Five or six times, smashing the victim's head on the concrete floor, just like this."

"Find him guilty," he asked again in a louder voice.

"This was no conspiracy of an investigation, as they would have you believe. Do you think two distinguished doctors would join in a prison conspiracy? Of course not."

Then he said something that made me so mad I wanted to stand up and object.

"Look at the bloody handprint on the sheet. Look at the bloody footprint next to the victim's body. The defendant can't wash that blood off."

I knew that he knew that the films showed that the bloody handprint was made by the nurse assisting Morris in my cell. The films showed that the bloody footprint was made by the men carrying him out on a stretcher. I hope Patterson rots in hell.

"Find him guilty of second-degree murder."

He turned to me. "The act of a *depraved* mind." He sat down.

Chapter 22

Trial for Another Murder:
Day 5
Jury Instructions

The judge gave the jury a break to recover from the closing arguments. Then she read them the lengthy jury instructions.

I tried to forget the state's closings. I thought Don did a terrific job. The jury hung on his every word, I thought. He's so believable and sincere.

I listened to the jury instructions pretty objectively. Overall, I thought the judge read a lot of stuff helpful to my defense. She went over reasonable doubt again. As Don had said in his closing argument, she read the part about an "abiding conviction of guilt" which must be put aside if you "waiver" or "vacillate." Those are great words for the defense. Who wouldn't "waiver" or "vacillate" with testimony from the likes of the guard, Crosby, or one look at those grainy black and white photos of me behind wire mesh, not even showing my injuries?

Next, she read the charge of second-degree murder. She emphasized that to find me guilty of that the jury would need to find evidence of a depraved state of mind, ill will in the relationship between me and Morris or intent. What relationship? Prison guards stick a raving lunatic into my cell where I have nothing to defend myself. Lock us up? Don't come back for hours? Where is the relationship here?

Finally, she read the lesser included offenses that the jury could find me guilty of even if they didn't convict me of second-degree murder. She read the definition for each: felony murder, manslaughter, aggravated battery, felony battery and battery. It just occurred to me then that neither the state nor my lawyers ever mentioned these lesser included offenses. I guess both sides were going for broke. Second-degree murder or acquittal.

Judge Hawthorne went over the verdict form with the jury. She told them the first thing they had to do was elect a foreperson. She told them that their verdict had to be unanimous, the verdict of each one of them and the verdict of the jury as a whole. She told them that if they had a question, they could write it down and give it to the bailiff, who would give it to her. She would then discuss it with the attorneys and either send a note back or bring them into the courtroom.

She asked the attorneys if she had read the jury instructions correctly. Of course they said yes. I guess this is for the record.

She sent the six members of the jury out to deliberate just before noon. Then she thanked the two alternates for their service and gave them certificates with a gold seal to hang on their walls. She told them they could talk to anyone who asked about the case now, and they were also free to refuse to talk to anyone. It was their choice.

The young Hispanic guy in the front row was one of the alternate jurors. Shit, I thought. I really liked him. I thought that of all the jurors he seemed most like me and would understand my case. Bad luck, I thought.

I wondered if the jurors were going to get lunch. I wondered if a quick verdict would be good or bad for us. I wondered if they would have a question. I wondered what I would do when this week was over and I was no longer part of a trial team in a courtroom with a judge and jury.

I wondered if I would ever again have advocates like Toby and Don standing in my corner and rooting for me. Defending me with everything they had and everything they knew. Standing up for Leo...Leo Lansing Boatman.

Chapter 23

Trial for Another Murder: Day 5

The Verdict

I thought I could wait in the courtroom with Toby and Don until the jury came back. I was wrong. My guards took me back to the side room and stayed with me. Toby and Don went to their office to catch up on other work. The bailiff had their phone numbers and would call them as soon as the jury reached a verdict. I saw Vic leave the courtroom. Today he had his friend Matt with him. I'd met him a few times when I lived with Vic in his trailer. I hoped they were going to a good place for lunch.

If you think waiting in a dentist's office is agony, or waiting for a check to arrive in the mail, it isn't anything compared to waiting for a jury to return a verdict. Now, it's not as bad as solitary confinement, that's for sure, but it is pure agony. I couldn't read the newspaper or a magazine. I couldn't concentrate. I guess everybody felt that way as Deputy Fox and the other three guards didn't have much to say either.

Except for one thing.

Deputy Fox took me aside. He said he thought I had a good chance at a not guilty verdict. He said he didn't think the state had proved its case. That made me feel good, but even more nervous. I didn't want to get too hopeful.

Then the jury had a question. We all filed into the courtroom again and waited for Judge Hawthorne. She read the jury's questions, which had to do with a definition of all of the charges, and with the lawyers' approval she sent a note back to them telling them to read the jury instructions again for an answer to their question. It was really all for nothing and it just made it more nerve wracking.

That word *depraved* stayed with me. I kept hearing it over and over. I couldn't get it out of my mind.

I thought of a lot of things during the four hours or so we waited until the jury reached a verdict. I thought of my grandmother. She tried hard with me. She'd had a tough life. So many kids to raise. Not much help from her husbands. Her worries about my mother. Then trying to raise Rosie and me. I wish I hadn't given her so much trouble. I'm glad she never lived to know that I murdered those college kids.

Now all I had were Rosie and Vic. Vic said he'd bring Rosie to the trial, but she didn't come. I called him collect from the jail one night and he told me she'd given him a fictitious address in Clearwater. He went to pick her up early one morning during the trial and she wasn't there. She'd never lived there. She didn't answer his phone calls. So, all that's left now really is Vic. I really appreciated that he came every day of the trial. He told me he had to borrow gas money and he and Matt used Matt's food stamps for lunch.

I played mind games with myself while I waited. I tried to look at my case in different ways, like lawyers do. In one respect, what the hell did it matter? To avoid a death sentence, I was serving life without parole. I'd agreed to it. My public defender, Bill Miller, in Ocala, worked hard to get that deal and I appreciated what he did and that the victims' families agreed to it.

But there was another side to the case.

I felt bad that I'd killed John Parker, who had a small child. I knew what it was like to grow up without a father. I wished I could do something for her. I felt bad that I killed Amber Peck. She was going to be a veterinarian. If I'd come home from the forest that day, maybe I would have completed classes to be a veterinarian technician. I was enrolled at St. Petersburg College. I was smart enough to finish.

Depraved.

I felt bad that people thought this way about me. I wanted to show people that I was just human. I wanted those prison officials to know what they did by putting a madman in my cell. I wanted my lawyers to feel victory, to think that I was worth defending.

Most of all, I wanted the jury to find that I wasn't *depraved.*

Four hours after the jury began their deliberations the bailiff told us they had reached a verdict.

Once again we all gathered in the courtroom. We waited for the judge. Once she took the bench, the bailiff brought the jury in.

"Your Uncle Vic told me he talked to the alternate juror, the Hispanic guy, when he left the courthouse," Toby whispered to me. "Vic said he told him that he would have found you not guilty. Vic said the guy said the state hadn't proved anything."

"Really," I said, trying not to show emotion.

"But don't give it much weight," Toby said. "Vic probably told the guy he was your uncle. Alternates don't participate in the deliberations. He probably told Vic what he thought Vic wanted to hear."

The jury now was seated, and Judge Hawthorne asked them if they'd reached a verdict. The foreperson said yes, and handed the verdict form to the bailiff, who gave it to the clerk, who gave it to the judge. Judge Hawthorne read the verdict— was this taking like a zillion minutes?—and then handed it to the clerk.

The clerk stood up, we stood up, and the clerk read:

"The State of Florida versus Leo Lancing Boatman."

My knees were shaking. I forced myself to look up.

"On the charge of second-degree murder, the jury finds the defendant, Leo Lancing Boatman, 'Not Guilty.'"

Author's note: The jury did find Leo Boatman guilty of a third degree felony that resulted in the death of Ricky Morris. Judge Hawthorne sentenced him to 15 years in prison, to be served concurrently with life without parole.

Chapter 24

Letter Written from Florida State Prison
January 23, 2011

Dear Judge Sullivan,

They're withholding my mail.

My mail is the only thing I get in solitary confinement. I can't have books. I can't have TV. I can't see other inmates. When another inmate walks by my cell, they close my outside door so I can't see him. When I go to recreation, it is by myself, to a cage the same size as my cell, only outside and with a dip bar, and only twice a month.

About two months ago, my mail just stopped. After two weeks I complained. I wrote it up. Well, that night, I got about 15 letters, all of them backdated. Four were from you, two were from Ken. Most were articles and stuff to keep me busy, but a few were from my sister. After five years, we are finally talking and she's writing me. I'm trying to rebuild my relationship with her, but it's hard to do when someone wants to play games with my mail.

So, after those 15 letters, another month and a half goes by, and I don't get any mail. Now I know something is wrong, so I begin to write request forms, then grievances. I talk to the sergeants on our wing, the people in charge, you name it. I do everything I'm supposed to do, but they just keep blowing me off. When I finally do get an answer, all they tell me is that the mail is delivered the same day they get it. That's a load of crap because I know something is wrong.

Well, finally, after a month and a half I get a letter from Archie. He's worried sick because he hasn't heard from me in so long. But I've been writing to him at least once a week! All this time I'm wondering if everyone has just forgotten me, or if they are all right, but I'm comforted by the fact that at least they are getting my letters. But now I find out that not only am I not getting my mail, I'm not being allowed to send out my mail either. And it's stressing Archie because he doesn't think I'm writing. He just had triple bypass surgery and doesn't need the stress. Plus, he's like a father to me and I sure could use the letters to help see me through.

So, I snap. But in a peaceful way. I covered my cell bars with my sheets so they could not see in my cell to do count. I told the sergeant, politely, that I needed to see a white shirt, because they are withholding my mail, and until I get my mail my sheets are not coming down. I told them it's all I got, it lets me know I exist, and if you take my mail, I cease to exist.

If they take away my mail, they might as well give me the death penalty. All I have is my mail. I'm not the nicest guy in the world. I deserve to be punished, but I never tortured anybody and I don't deserve to be tortured. I feel pain and I cry out when it's too much to bear.

Well, the white shirt comes, but he doesn't even try to find out what the problem is. He just tries to rip my sheets down. I, of course, stop that and he laughs, egging me on, saying, 'Is that all you've got?' What the Hell? I never caused you no problems. I never asked you for anything and I've got a serious problem. But this is what I get. So, obviously peace is not understood in prison. Peaceful protests are worth nothing.

When I continue to keep my sheets up, they just start gassing me. Can after can. Eventually I had to come out because I couldn't breathe. But they put me in again and turned on my sprinkler and once again I refused to come out. So, they gassed me again. I told them I'd continue to do this no matter what they did to me until I got my mail.

What do you know? I got 14 letters on January 19th, that day. Now keep in mind that they continued to deny I had any mail until then. Then they claimed that the state attorney had it as part of my investigation. OK, so they went all the way to Charlotte County and picked it up? That was obviously a lie. Even if (which I'm sure it is) my mail is under review, it is not supposed to be withheld for so long. When it comes here, the inspectors are supposed to copy it, then send me my letter. They were just getting lazy and throwing my mail to the side until they could get to it. I had to go through all that to get my mail and it was here all along. What's more, isn't my mail protected by Federal law?

They wrote me SIX! Disciplinary referrals for just that one day. They kind of know how to push our buttons so then they can write you up and justify keeping you back here in solitary confinement.

Well, I'd appreciate it if you did not share this with Archie because he'd just worry. And I'm sorry if I bored you, or if you don't want to hear my whining. It feels good to unburden myself though. Hopefully this will get to you, but there's a chance you may never even get this letter. I have to wonder how you will respond. You were a judge, so I'm sure you have a strong sense of law and punishment, of justice and what not. But do we stop being human after our crime for the rest of our lives?

I'll write more soon. I'd normally wait for a response but who knows when I'll get that.

Hope all is well,
Leo

"I'm not asking for forgiveness or pity.
I just want to tell my story so that what happened to me
never happens to another foster child again."

Leo Boatman

Leo at trial

PART 3

Chapter 25

Author's Note: Visiting Leo

I took a detour through Silver Springs and the entrance to the Ocala National Forest on my drive to visit Leo Boatman at Florida State Prison in Raiford. Driving east on Highway 40, which becomes single lane about fifteen miles out of Ocala, takes you back in time and not just because you lose cell phone service for a bit. You drive past the local businesses that cater to boaters, campers and hikers who enjoy the beautiful pine forest. You won't find chain restaurants or hotels. Rather, you drive past Sparks Place, the Dollar General, the Blackwater Inn on the St. Johns River, Steel Around Tavern, a VFW post, laundromat, tiny Chamber of Commerce and a First Baptist Church.

I stopped at the Juniper Springs entrance to the forest, where Leo camped out and waited for a ranger to open the gate that fateful morning. I couldn't get out of my head the tragedy that occurred, the loss of Amber Peck and John Parker, who had everything going for them and everything ahead of them. But for Leo. Unlike Leo.

The Big House, as the prison is known, is a massive cream-colored concrete block structure surrounded by chain link and barbed wire in a flat open field devoid of large trees or vegetation. It is easy to reach the visitor parking lot. It gets a lot harder after that.

My appointment to see Leo had to be scheduled two weeks in advance. He was allowed two visitors every two weeks. I called to confirm the visit with Ms. Maddox, his classification officer, who provided specific instructions.

I stopped outside the massive steel fences that surrounded the main building to catch the attention of the officer in the large control tower. He or she buzzed me in through two different sets of motorized gates that opened and closed after I entered. Once inside, I saw children seated outside the visitor check in, waiting for their mothers to present identification, surrender a driver's license and register the family in for the visit. I did the same, and we all proceeded through airport-type security, including a pat down. In the next corridor, handprints were taken and matched to the prisoner's pin number.

Following that, the eight kids, three mothers and I were led to a small canteen where we could order food for the inmate to eat during the visit, and food for ourselves if we wished. The choice is fairly broad: chicken wings, cheeseburgers, pizzas, sandwiches, soft drinks, candy and ice cream. It was very inexpensive. Most of it was frozen and had to be heated in what seemed to be the first microwave ever invented, it was so old and slow. The mothers told me to be patient and joked that, even frozen, the snacks were so much better than prison food that the inmates didn't mind. One large family spent over forty dollars on hot food for all of them to enjoy, as well as the father.

After the food was heated, we were led to a narrow room with 12 heavy glass windows and folding chairs placed in front of them for seating. The guard took the food to the prisoners, and we took our seats before the window in front of the prisoner we were visiting. There is no way to touch the prisoner and no phone or microphone to amplify a voice. Only a thick glass window with a tiny tin slot in the middle to speak into. When the room is full, as it was on my visit, you have to shout to be heard, and the inmate has to shout as well. You can imagine how little can be understood when the narrow room is filled with visitors all shouting to be heard.

Leo smiled at me. His head was shaved, his face was thin, and he said he had lost weight on the diet of soy products dressed up as meat. He said they had real chicken once a week, a day he looked forward to. As I watched him eat his snacks, I could tell from the gestures he made, pointing to his teeth, that the cheeseburgers and chicken wings hadn't fully thawed.

"Next time you visit, get two Angus cheeseburgers with pepper jack cheese, one pizza, and ice cream cookie, four Skittles, a bag of gummy bears and an orange soda," he shouted at me. "Forget the chicken wings."

He told me that his former court-appointed guardian, Archie, had recently visited. "It was the first time I'd seen him in almost ten years," he said, adding that Archie writes to him often. "Don't throw him under the bus when you write the book," he warned. "He's the only one that's stuck with me. When you're out of my life, he will still be around."

I watched the children to my left and right shout at their fathers, soon becoming bored or tired of the effort. I watched them sit silently as their mothers took over the conversation. Some of them were Leo's age when he was first molested by Archie. How lonely or desperate did you have to become to want your abuser as a friend?

I actually had little to say to Leo under these circumstances. His letters were much more informative than this public visit could ever be. I could tell he was impatient, trying to shout at me. I wondered why telephone handsets couldn't be installed.

Privacy, I gathered, is not a priority in prison.

Enroute home, I drove through one of the many fast-food places in nearby Starke and bit into a double cheeseburger, which came to me steamy warm in its foil wrapper. I thought of Leo, the frozen snacks and the soy meals. I thought of the children I had been with, visiting their fathers in prison. Trying to talk to them, to enjoy a meal with them, despite the glass between them.

I thought of Leo, aging out of juvenile prison and foster care at age nineteen, with free college tuition and a monthly stipend from the state. Good things, but not a word of guidance, a mentor, or any positive role models.

Then I thought of Amber Peck and John Parker, no longer able to complete their education, and their families, no longer able to be with them, because of Leo.

Chapter 26

His Past Became His Predator
Adele Solazzo, PhD,
Clinical Psychologist

I met with Leo over closed circuit TV in the Charlotte County Jail in the summer of 2013. I also had the opportunity to review his entire history of child abuse, juvenile imprisonment, release and the subsequent tragic murders in the Ocala National Forest.

There is no boundary that has not been breached in Leo's life. Sexual abuse by adults he should have trusted, physical abuse, neglect and abandonment characterized his youth. He was victimized time and time again throughout his life. He quickly began to adopt the approach of brutalizing others before he himself was brutalized.

Leo notes that the trauma and abuse he experienced was documented in his dependency file. Yet there is a disconnect between noting the trauma and effectively intervening. In fact, Leo appears to have been placed in situation after situation where he was repeatedly re-traumatized. There is often either a diffusion of responsibility or a lack of ownership of difficulties with many children who are in care. Problems are noted, placements are changed, but there are minimal efforts to "fix" or take care of the needs of the child via treatment. The passing along of the problem, combined with frequent changes of case managers, often leaves children like Leo with no one to advocate for their best interests. Even one person providing a steady and safe relationship is often enough to overcome significant adversity.

In the early years, before he entered Tony's foster care home, the adults who sexually abused him were primarily in parental roles. His poly victimization has resulted in lifelong trauma that plays a large part in his destructive and impulsive behavior. Leo's pathway of poly victimization started with a dangerous home environment where there was a significant family adversity coupled with neighborhoods/placements that were vulnerable to abuse. His family and community situation set the stage for abuse. He began to develop emotional and behavioral problems that caused him to be a burden for his grandmother. Her withdrawal, both physically and emotionally, led him to even more vulnerability. Leo's victimization and exposure to multiple other traumas had a significant and long-term impact on his ability to self-regulate his behavior. His anxiety, aggression, defiance, impulsivity, destructive behaviors, feelings of hopelessness, guilt and shame can be traced to his complex and abusive experiences.

The fundamental aspect of growing up is to develop self-regulation. Leo's ongoing victimization with important adults in his life has led to attachment issues and a subsequent loss of his ability to regulate his behavior. Leo's maltreatment was complicated by his poly victimization. There is no record of anyone who was responsible for Leo's care that noticed how his emotional, behavioral and interpersonal problems were adaptations he made to survive his complex traumas.

Leo would like professionals working with children in similar circumstances to think, "They are acting out for a reason." Leo's perception of others focusing on his outward behavior and not seeing the trigger for behavioral issues was a continual obstacle in his life. Many clinicians tie the origin of Conduct Disorder to past traumas. In court evaluations, the combination Mood Disorder NOS, ADHD, and Oppositional Defiant Disorder/Conduct Disorder represent a type of code for a youth who has experienced chronic trauma. It's significant that the school system labeled him severely emotionally disturbed at age ten.

Leo is the victim of sexual abuse by his mother since early childhood. His words describing the abuse are devoid of emotion, almost clinical. He compartmentalized the abuse. In Leo's case, the sexual abuse is different from many other cases, both because one of the perpetrators was his mother and because there were numerous and diverse perpetrators.

Sexual abuse by mothers is rare. These mothers are often diagnosed with a psychotic disorder or other severe mental health disorder. Leo takes away the blame for the abuse, writing, "no one understood" his mother—minimizing her role and responsibility. He felt his mother's head injury had changed her personality to the point that she could not be held responsible for her actions. Leo focuses on a fantasy of his birth that involves his mother looking at him lovingly. This moment is the only normal interaction with his mother that he reports. His fantasy provides him with comfort and the sense that he was once loved as a precious child.

However, the fantasy also leads him to think about his father. He is horrified about the choices he has about his father. Leo struggles with the question of "who is my father?" What he does not discuss but is clearly impacted by is "how much am I like my father?"

It is notable that Leo's other father images, Greg and Archie, also have sexual connotations and abuse. Leo falls into the substrate of poly victimization where he was abused by both his mother and by his father figures. While he does not report any outright abuse concerning Greg, the implication is that when he refused to share Greg's bed, he was yanked out of the home. Archie, whom he refers to as "Dad," had frequent sexual relations with Leo. Leo is very protective of these men and has compartmentalized their roles that include a sexual aspect as well as a more normal parental role; for example, caring for him when he was sick, taking him on trips, fishing and buying him gifts. Leo is reluctant to acknowledge Archie's sexual abuse. He is very concerned that Archie does not get into trouble for those acts. Archie is one of only two or three people that visit Leo. He would do anything not to jeopardize his visits or letters. These visits provide his only sense of connection to the outside world. He does not trust or have a relationship with fellow inmates. He obtains a semblance of positive human interaction through visits and letters.

His grandmother's physical abuse and maltreatment and eventual abandonment of him added to the series of ongoing psychological injuries. He admires his grandmother for the difficult life she led. His loyalty and defensiveness of his family is a common response in abused children. Attacking those abusive family members is like attacking a very vulnerable part of him. He has forgiven the past abuse. These ongoing traumas and the past traumas have resulted in a fragmented sense of self over which he does not have good control.

Leo's abuse by peers and other caregivers became a normal way of life for him, although he does not discuss his behaviors other than to say that maybe he was "a little hyperactive" during the time he lived with his grandmother. The years of incarceration in programs, now closed for abusive practices, wore him down. Feelings of humanity dissipated while feelings of vengeance and rage became more pronounced. He was traumatized again and again on top of a lifetime of abuse. Leo's behavior became more destructive and aggressive because other behavioral options produced minimal results in his circumstances.

Looking back, Leo believes that the time he spent in the group home with Tony was one of the two worst placements in his life. He felt devalued as a person—his wishes and feelings were not important. He remembers calling the abuse line to report the abuse in the home, only to be more thoroughly beaten when the allegations were deemed unfounded. He describes monthly meetings with his psychiatrist, where Tony was the one to describe Leo's behavior and what medications were working best. Leo's input was disregarded. Being under the control of someone who was cruel to him encouraged feelings of helplessness and hopelessness to grow. Eventually the outward expression of those feelings would cost him his freedom for the rest of his life.

By the time he was discharged from the commitment facility, he had no personal sense of normal familial or other peer relationships. He had minimal skills to be successful. He writes that assistance post discharge was obtained because he looked up programs and demanded help. Transition planning to community life was not provided by those "parental figures" that were in charge of his care.

Leo projects blame for many of his behavior onto others in his writings. After his release from commitment, he talks about the accident with the motorcycle being "Vic's fault." Vic did not take the time to teach him how to ride. Leo did not perceive his behavior—riding the motorcycle without adequate instruction—as the primary reason for the accident. He perceives his actions as reactions to the behavior of others. He talks about his sister coming sporadically. She will visit one month and then maybe not visit again for another six months. He became angry when he said to me: "I do everything I am supposed to do. Follow the rules, not get into trouble and then she does not come. I earned the visit."

It is difficult for Leo to understand that his sister's drug abuse issues, her own trauma, or even financial issues might be obstacles to visiting as opposed to his behavior. He acknowledges that he may have been sanctioned more frequently with solitary confinement during times when visits were scarce. This situation is another example where he has difficulty owning up to his responsibility but rather sees his behavior as a response to perceived injustice or unfairness.

Although Leo is an individual with minimal education who grew up in abusive circumstances, he is articulate and is able to express his views logically and eloquently. The fantasy for the reader is to imagine how an engaging and intelligent young man could have turned out differently if someone responsible for his care addressed his trauma and provided a safe place.

Leo participates in "Scared Straight" programs offered at the prison where youth at risk of entering deeper into the delinquency system listen to convicted offenders. Although this type of program has limited efficacy, Leo enjoys the interaction. He states the message he gives to others who are at risk for criminal behavior is "Do what is best for you. Don't let yourself be controlled by anger you feel toward someone." Leo believes this advice, but it has been hard advice for him to follow. He has been placed in solitary confinement many times due to angry reactions. He continues to become easily agitated if he perceives that he is being treated unfairly.

Leo has thought about the brutal murders of Amber Peck and John Parker many times in the past seven years. He talks of waking up that day in a "strange mood that I couldn't shake." He describes a type of disassociation where he was thinking of his past abuse and not the shooting and disposal of two bodies—bodies of people who were helpful and kind to him in passing. In essence, Leo's past became his predator.

Leo's return to Vic's home after the murders and attending college classes are further examples of his ability to compartmentalize his behaviors. But, on that sunny, hot Florida summer day in Charlotte County Jail, Leo said without hesitation that he takes full responsibility for the murders. He was able to verbalize that there was nothing he could do or could say that would make up for the loss of life and the pain suffered by John and Amber's families and friends.

When I visited him, Leo was awaiting sentencing for a crime that occurred while he was incarcerated for that double homicide. As noted in this book, a violent inmate who had just grievously wounded an older inmate was mistakenly placed in Leo's cell instead of in solitary confinement. This inmate attacked Leo, who responded with a rage that killed the other inmate. While he accepts his accountability for John and Amber's murder, he is vehement in not accepting responsibility for this inmate's death. The court found him guilty of a felony leading to a death, but not second-degree murder. Leo took satisfaction in that ruling. However, he became a bit more uncomfortable when we explored the depth of his violent response. He did not stop at subduing the other inmate. The autopsy report shows that the inmate's head was slammed into the concrete multiple times, and his ear was partially torn off. He was hesitantly able to acknowledge that although he had a right to defend himself, his response was significantly more violent than was necessary. The anger, the rage of a lifetime of mistreatment, continues to be easily triggered.

Leo is where he needs to be. His inability to regulate his emotions and the subsequent impulsivity, aggression and danger he poses is too much of a risk for society. His destruction of two innocent lives is a crime for which he must be held accountable during his life sentence. However, it is important for us to understand how he arrived at that place and how failure of the system to provide adequate care and safeguards has a role in the man he became.

It is encouraging that Leo wants to be liked. He is intelligent and wants to learn. He is dismayed that he was not the one to close down the abusive settings in the foster home or at Omega Juvenile Prison. He was just a victim of those placements. Although Leo owes a debt to society for those murders, we owe Leo something as well. Acknowledge his trauma. Provide him with the education he so desperately wants. Allow him access to counseling. Give him the chance to make a difference in his setting. The alternative is a continuous buildup of resentment and anger. He brutalizes others first to avoid being brutalized. The potential for destruction to life by inmates during a lifetime sentence is huge. Perhaps it is time to change our approach to Leo Boatman and give him tools to change so he can be a positive addition to the prison system and not the name synonymous with senseless murder.

Chapter 27

Snap

Kenneth Wooden, Investigative Journalist and Author of *Weeping in the Playtime of Others—America's Incarcerated Children*

When I met Leo face to face in a small prison room, I instantly recognized him. He was the composite of thousands of juveniles I visited, spoke with and wrote about in my first book, *Weeping in the Playtime of Others—America's Incarcerated Children.* And, like Leo Boatman, their entry into the penal system wasn't for crimes. Society and the justice system just didn't know what to do with them. Nor did the political system care. So, these children became fodder for an economic industry that provided lucrative contracts and public jobs on the backs and dreams of young kids like Leo, who had committed crimes but paid a terrible price for society's crimes against its youth.

In 1977, I testified before Congress. "Juvenile incarceration is a billion-dollar business, and they need lots of kids to make that kind of money." Thirty-two years later, in Luzerne County, Pennsylvania, Judges Mark Ciavarella and Michael T. Conahan, pleaded guilty to receiving $2.6 million in pay-offs for committing juveniles to lockup. Law enforcement confiscated a yacht the judges owned in Florida called REEL JUSTICE. Both were sentenced to many years in Federal prison and ordered to pay almost $1 million in restitution.

Sexual assault of children and youth is the Great American Taboo. Massachusetts Institute of Technology students recently labeled "the heavy silence surrounding sexual violence on campus—the elephant in the room." It is a chilling echo of the 1995 declaration by the American Medical Association that rape of children and women is "a violent, silent epidemic." In 2013, news reporting documented that sexual abuse and exploitation of children and teens continues virtually unabated today.

It has been said many times that the Last Frontier of Human Rights will be safeguarding the human rights of children. The heart-wrenching tragedy in Newtown, Connecticut, may finally place that last frontier front and center before the conscience of our country. And we would be remiss to ignore the recurring relationship between such violence and sexual violence against children and youth. What happens to children who suffer abuse, neglect and sexual exploitation, and are not then given proper attention, mental health counseling, help or love? It depends. Leo Boatman, who shot and killed two college students in Central Florida, Charles Manson ("Helter Skelter") and Perry Edward Smith ("In Cold Blood") all experienced the trauma and degradation of repeated sexual assaults and physical beatings as they grew from childhood into adulthood.

Charles Manson summed up his own disturbing childhood to me: "You have seen me in the eyes of eleven-year-olds. I was just an early warning." To the detriment of society, many mental health experts fail to publicly correlate untreated childhood sexual trauma with rage in young adults. Rage that can ultimately lead to violence against themselves or others.

Research unequivocally documents that childhood trauma has lifelong consequences. This is particularly true if the child is sexually abused—like Boatman, Manson and Smith—in what should be a nurturing and supportive environment, be it home, foster home, school, club, faith-based facility, treatment center or correctional facility. Lack of proper mental health treatment can leave young victims of sexual crimes far more vulnerable to depression, substance abuse, eating disorders, poor school performance, school dropout, self harm, prostitution, crime and arrests. At worst, it can lead to suicide and, for a small number of victims, to violent rage directed at others.

Despite the system, some kids are saved. I personally intervened for one young man convicted of selling marijuana by appealing to the federal judge for leniency in sentencing. Chris Bianco is now meaningfully employed and a loving husband and father. He was fortunate in that there were many others supporting him at a critical time. His life was redeemed, allowing him to reach out with love and kindness to other human beings. This was not the case for Malcolm Robbins, a child-killer I interviewed as an investigative reporter for ABC News 20/20 for a segment called "The Lures of Death." As a youngster, Malcolm walked in the same shoes as Leo Boatman.

Malcolm grew up in Portland, Maine. His mother was a prostitute, and when her customers were finished with her, they often came into the young boy's room and raped him. Malcolm thought they were showing him affection. Like Leo Boatman, Malcolm Robbins was eventually swept into the state's protective services/juvenile justice system. After being repeatedly raped in juvenile prison, he attempted suicide, using wires he tore from a light fixture. Failing to take his own life, Robbins later used wire to snuff out the lives of five boys in California, Texas, West Virginia and New Jersey.

We see this cycle of violence over and over again—from the likes of the Boston Strangler (Albert DeSalvo) and Charles Manson to obscure criminals like Leo Boatman, Malcolm Robbins, and youngsters across America who, armed with automatic weapons, lash out against parents, siblings, classmates, teachers and complete strangers. A case in point was buried in a lengthy 1998 New York Times article concerning Paula Jones and the Clinton sex scandal. A leading Arkansas citizen, Jack Walls, had been sent to prison for molesting children in his Boy Scout troop and community of Lonoke, Arkansas. One of his victims, twelve-year-old Heath Stocks, had shot and killed his parents and sister the year before in 1997. Although law enforcement authorities estimate Jack

Walls abused over 150 children in Lonoke, Arkansas, he had not been identified through Boy Scouts of America in their now public "Perversion Files" of over 20,000 names.

Face-to-face with Leo in that small, stark prison room, I asked him what filled his thoughts during the prolonged periods of time he spent in solitary confinement at Omega Juvenile Prison for institutional infractions. He said he dwelt, with growing hatred, on the guards who taunted him for being too weak to fight off older boys who raped him and their enjoyment discussing such sexual acts between young inmates. The guards would read aloud from Leo's file about his mother giving birth to him in "a nut house," and Leo never knowing who his father was. And then there were the betrayals by men (guardians and father figures) who said they loved him, only to betray him by using him sexually.

According to Leo, though, the bulk of his time in the hole was devoted to two very long, re-occurring fantasies. One was positive: "Being free on the outside...alone, enjoying nature, walking in the woods, hunting and fishing in its streams and camping out under the stars by a fire." The other, a more constant and dark fantasy, was "hiding outside a guard's home, behind bushes, and watching through a window as his kids decorate the Christmas tree. Then, killing the guard so the kids would grow up without a father, like me."

If one reconstructs the crime scene at Hidden Pond in Ocala National Park during January of 2006, it is apparent that Boatman's two recurring fantasies—camping out in the great outdoors and later hiding in bushes with a firearm, waiting to kill—merged and ended in the cold-blooded murder of two innocent college students. Leo Boatman snapped like Charles Manson, Perry Edwards, Malcolm Robbins, and the Boy Scout from a little town in Arkansas, Heath Stock, and a host of similar, angry, traumatized survivors. Without intervention and support, it is possible that some of today's victims (especially those with access to weapons) are at great risk of making tomorrow's headlines.

Common sense tells us that if a human being is treated with basic respect and love, they will usually respond by blossoming into a decent, productive member of society. If, however, indifference, neglect or physical/mental/sexual abuse is perpetrated on a child like Leo Boatman, the outcome can be reflected in the poetry of Langston Hughes:

> What happens to a dream deferred?
> Does it dry up
> like a raisin in the sun?
> Does it fester like a sore
> And then run?
> Or does it explode?

Can we as a nation break free of our complacency toward the "violent, silent epidemic," of which the AMA warned us nearly twenty years ago? Or, with deliberate indifference, will we cowardly allow more troubled individuals to snap like Leo and the twelve-year-old boy scout from Arkansas? For the millions of survivors of childhood abuse who suffer in long silence, we owe it to them, ourselves and tomorrow's children to prevent childhood sexual abuse and to ensure that abused children and youth receive the mental health treatment they need to heal and thrive.

At the end of our interview, Leo Boatman and I both stood. There was a long pause of silence. I was thinking of all those solitary confinement cells I had visited during my years of research; the names, the dates, the messages that were scratched, carved, or gouged into metal or dirty concrete walls. The frequently etched word that always tears at my core intellect is the four-letter word, "HELP," which so many institutionalized kids left as a mark for all to see. For kids like Leo Boatman, a lifeline to help does not exist.

My parting words were, "Leo, I wish I could have been your dad when you were a little kid."

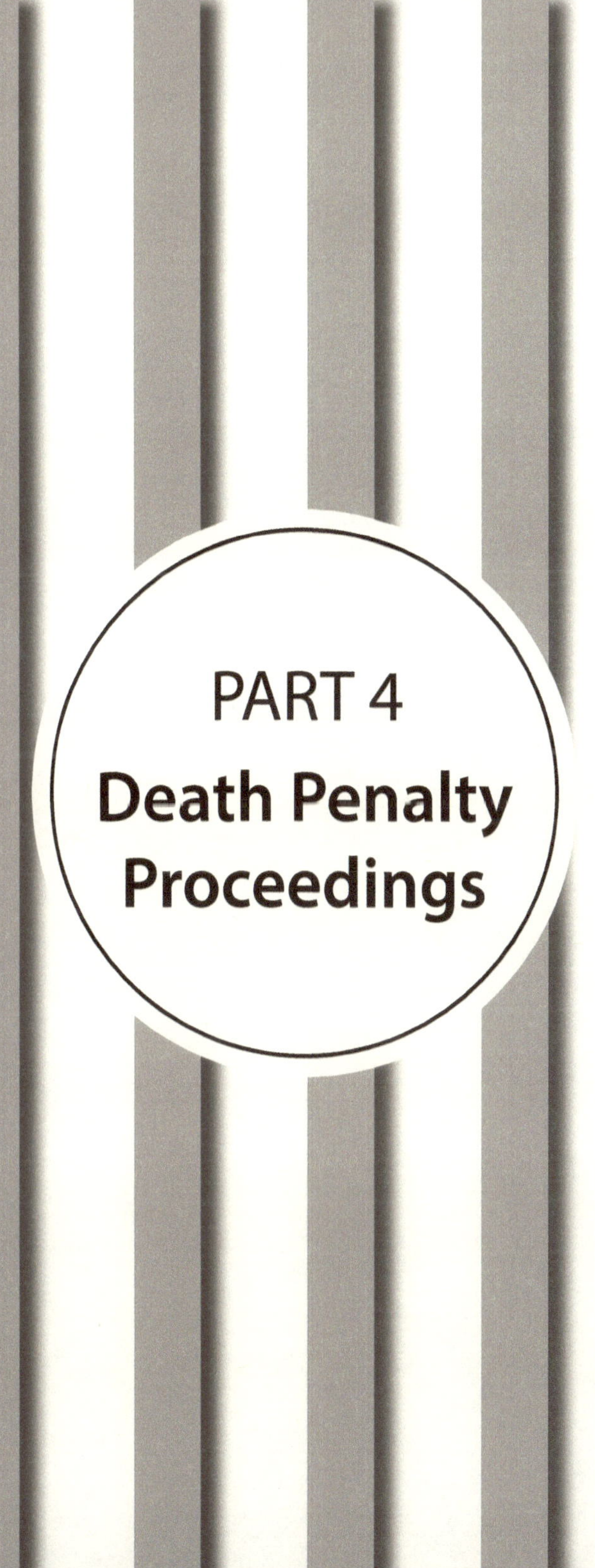

PART 4

Death Penalty
Proceedings

Chapter 28

Bradford County Courthouse, Florida
August 12, 2020

"Death is Different," Florida Circuit Judge Susan Schaeffer taught to new judges across the country as the expert on how to apply the death penalty. "Do it right the first time," she said, "so that it doesn't come back on appeal and you have to do it again—agony for the victim's family as well as the defendant."

I couldn't help but think that Circuit Judge Mark W. Moseley certainly had her words in mind as he tapped his gavel promptly at 2 p.m. on a sweltering day in north Florida. He smiled slightly at the masked men standing in front of him, then nodded at them to take their seats. They fully complied with Covid-19 safety precautions, sitting a few feet apart from one another. Boatman was charged with another murder of a prison inmate.

Public Defender Kristofer Eisenmenger introduced his client. "We are here to have the Court declare Leo Boatman incompetent to proceed. The State is not consenting but is not seeking a second competency evaluation [to determine whether Boatman has sufficient understanding to make the decision for himself]."

"Put your expert on the stand, then," Judge Moseley ordered, waving to the witness box on his left.

Dr. Tonia Werner raised her right hand, swore to tell the truth as she had dozens of times before, and looked straight at

Leo Boatman as she described the 96-minute meeting she had with him, her review of the case file and earlier records. "We discussed his birth, failed adoption, years in juvenile detention between the time he was returned to his grandmother, who returned him to his mother.

"We discussed his recent suicide attempts—some attention seeking and some sincerely intending to end his life."

Leo stared straight ahead when attorney Eisenmenger asked the doctor if she had a diagnosis. *Diagnosis, shit,* he thought. *I plead guilty to first degree murder. I want the death penalty. I want to live the best life I can have in here, which is on death row.*

Judge Moseley bent toward the petite doctor, adjusting his pen and notepad towards her, intent on what she had to say.

"Leo Boatman has a DSM 5 diagnosis, basically an adjustment disorder, depression, acting out, and identifiable stressors, such as being on closed management in prison. He recalls a traumatic childhood, juvenile detention, having to live in a closet.

"As to competency?" Eisenmenger inquired.

"He wants to be declared competent. He has made a decision to accept the death penalty. But it is not rational, as he is requesting the death penalty solely to get out of the closed management situation in prison. I find him incompetent to proceed because he is looking for relief from stressors, from closed management in prison, which is confining. He is seeking the death penalty to get out of it."

Judge Moseley remembered the case well as that the Court had ordered the mental evaluation when Leo Boatman first entered a plea to first degree murder to the "unprovoked, vicious murder of another inmate, for which the State of Florida was seeking the death penalty." The judge listened to Dr. Werner, the only expert to be called, to determine for himself whether Leo Boatman was competent to make this decision.

"The defendant meets the criteria for hospitalization

within the Department of Corrections," Dr. Werner concluded. "Removing him from closed management within the prison would help, as well as treating him with psychotherapy."

The state attorney jumped to his feet, eager to cross examine Dr. Werner.

"Leo Boatman does *not* meet the criteria for hospitalization, except for a setting within the Department of Corrections, right?"

"Right," she answered.

"When he met with you, he gave you no immediate suicidal ideations, right?"

"Right," she answered.

"He understood first degree murder, plea options, death sentence versus life sentence, the roles of the jury and the judge, and his ability to testify, right?"

"Yes," she admitted.

"So, if the decision was a trial rather than a plea, would he be competent?"

"It's not that simple. He pled guilty to get out of closed management. He wants to be on death row because for the last 13 years he has been an inmate at Florida State Prison. It's not necessarily to die, but to be on death row."

Judge Moseley interrupted. "I don't understand. Has this defendant considered the rationality of a plea for life without parole, as to a death row plea out of closed management? Is that not a rational choice? There is overwhelming evidence as to the nature of his guilt. I have seen it on video. He is already serving a life sentence. Isn't it a rational choice to enter the plea that he has?"

Dr. Werner responded: "The analogy is to be unable to walk and a doctor says I can give you something to enable you to walk that will shorten your life. It's not a free choice because of the pressure to accept being able to walk."

Judge Moseley asked again. "Does he have any delusions, voices, psychosis or symptoms like that?"

"No."

"So it's solely to escape the confinement he is held in?"

"Yes."

The state attorney spoke again. "Even through appeals and a few years before any death, he prefers the risk of a shorter life than a longer life, right?"

"It's still no free choice," Dr. Werner answered, "Even though he understands."

Public Defender Eisenmenger broke in. "He obviously feels pressure to get out of his present housing in prison. The only way out is to plead for death. This is disproportionate because of his history of trauma, sexual abuse, mental abuse, etc."

"I have to decide whether the circumstances driving Mr. Boatman's choice make it a rational choice. If it acts like a duck, swims like a duck and quacks like I duck, I can't find it's a chicken! Not wanting to spend the rest of your life in prison [in closed management] is not necessarily irrational," the judge concluded.

Listening in to the hearing, I sensed how Judge Moseley would rule. I wondered whether his rejection of the only expert opinion brought before him would create grounds for an appeal. I'd heard he had a reputation for making up his mind before rulings; however, he wasn't known for favoring either the prosecution or defense. He continued to explain his rationale:

"I can consider his background in terms of mitigation when the ultimate decision for sentencing comes to me. But I find now that he is competent, he knows the outcome, he understands the process and can discuss it rationally with his public defender. He has always manifested appropriate court-room behavior. There are no delusions here; the devil is not telling him.

"This is the essence of free will," Judge Moseley concluded. "Yes, he is under the stress of closed management, but in choosing this path he is quite frankly making a rational decision. Thus, I find Mr. Boatman competent to proceed."

Leo Boatman smiled. But Public Defender Kristofer Eisenmenger closed the hearing with his announcement to the judge:

"I can't support his plea for the death penalty. I can't advocate that for him or represent him in that matter."

Leo Boatman was escorted back to Florida State Prison in Starke, Florida, in closed management, essentially solitary confinement, until the next hearing to decide whether a jury or judge would sentence him to die.

"Death is Different"—and this was certainly a different kind of death case.

Chapter 29

Indictment of Leo Boatman

On November 4, 2019, the Bradford County Grand Jury indicted Leo Boatman and William Wells for the first-degree murder of William Chapman, a fellow inmate at Florida State Prison.

The state contends that Leo murdered Chapman in an act of revenge against prison authorities. Leo told me it was a reckless and impulsive act carried out to be sentenced to death because the living conditions on death row were better than those in maximum security. Either way, prison guards were negligent for leaving a number of violent prisoners unsupervised in a small day room while those prisoners waited their turns to use the internet for emails.

Video evidence of the murder and medical testimony established that Chapman died of multiple stab wounds to his body, internal injuries and strangulation. Chapman was basically stabbed, stomped and strangled to death while guards watched helplessly outside the waiting room that Leo Boatman and William Wells had jammed shut. Both defendants had made shanks and ligatures out of prison equipment, hiding them until that morning when they used them to murder Chapman in the dayroom.

Kristofer W. Eisenmenger, one of the fine public defenders appointed to represent Leo, convinced Leo that his life should be spared and that the disparity between death row and maximum-security living conditions should be addressed.

* * *

In the late summer of 2022, Leo's public defender, Kris Eisenmenger and I prepared the mitigation evidence required by law to be presented to spare a convicted first-degree murderer of a death sentence. I was the obvious choice as I had obtained Leo's early life, foster care and delinquency files. I knew his life story and I was eager to testify to it to spare his life.

On the witness box in the north Florida courthouse in Starke, Florida, I looked at Leo, at the defense table, looking handsome and well-groomed in a sport jacket and tie furnished by his attorneys. We nodded each other and I remember again the first words Leo told me when we met: "I want to tell my story so that what happened to me never happens to another foster kid."

I'd never testified before a jury so I was nervous. They know Leo had been found guilty of first-degree murder, so their decision today was life without parole, which Leo was already serving, or death. My job, as a witness for the defense, was to convince them to render a verdict for life without parole. I had plenty of evidence to support it.

As I began to testify about Leo's horrific life circumstances and the physical, sexual and mental abuse perpetrated upon him by his mother, her boyfriends, his grandmother, foster parents, the guardian ad litem and the prison guard, I saw the twelve jurors connecting with me and accepting my testimony. Leo's sister also testified to his horrible childhood. I thought the two of us had convinced at least one juror to spare Leo's life. That is all it took under Florida law at the time, as a verdict for death had to be unanimous.

Shortly after, I received a message from Kris, Leo's good attorney, that Leo had asked for the jury to be dismissed so that the Honorable James M. Colaw, the sentencing judge, could render a verdict instead of the jury. He certainly had the right to do that.

A bit later I received the following email from Kris:

From: "Kristofer W. Eisenmenger"
To: "Irene"
Cc:
Sent: Wednesday November 9 2022 7:39:56PM
Subject: Leo Boatman Sentencing

Irene,

It is with deep sorrow that I write to inform you that Judge Colaw has sentenced Leo to death. I fully believe we would have prevailed with a jury and thank you for all of your assistance in this case. The small bright spot in this dark day is that Leo may finally be released from confinement in max management and be granted the privileges of death row inmates. I have attached Judge Colaw's sentencing order. I am still digesting it but please know that I disagree with very many things within.

-Kris

Chapter 30

The Sentencing Order

IN THE CIRCUIT COURT OF
THE EIGHTH JUDICIAL CIRCUIT
IN AND FOR BRADFORD COUNTY, FLORIDA
STATE OF FLORIDA,
Plaintiff,
CASE NO.: 04-2019-CF-000706-B
VS.
LEO LANCING BOATMAN,
Defendant.
SENTENCING ORDER

This Order is entered pursuant to section 921.141 (3) and (4), Florida Statutes. on November 4, 2019, the Defendant, Leo L. Boatman, was indicted for First-Degree Murder by the Bradford County Grand Jury for the death of William L. Chapman, as well as possession of a weapon by a state prisoner. The State filed its Notice of Intent to Seek the Death Penalty on December 3, 2019.

On August 19, 2022, the Defendant was found guilty after a jury trial of First-Degree Murder (count I) and Possession of a Weapon by a State Prisoner (count II) as alleged in the Indictment.

On August 22, 2022, the penalty phase trial began. During the penalty phase trial, the Defendant chose to waive the jury for the remainder of the proceeding and, ultimately, have the court determine the appropriate sentence. Multiple colloquies were conducted with the Defendant on his decision. The Court additionally had the Defendant talk with a psychiatrist who was a defense witness; and who had previously evaluated him for competency. Further, the Court deliberated on the Defendant's request while the penalty phase continued with the jury. After

———————————————————————

SENTENCING ORDER
STATE VS. LEO LANCING BOATMAN
CASE No. 04-2019-CF-000706-B
PAGE 2

substantial deliberation and considering the Defendant's statements to the Court as to the reasons for his decision, the court permitted the Defendant to waive the jury sentence determination.

A special hearing was conducted during the penalty phase hearing with the Court. Both the State and Defendant had an opportunity to present additional evidence to the Court. The Court has heard and considered the evidence presented in both the guilt phase and the penalty phase of the trial as well as the evidence presented at the special hearing. The Court has also considered and reviewed the sentencing memoranda filed by both sides, and the case-law cited therein.

The Court has fully examined the evidence, testimony, and all other matters in this case regarding the presence of or lack of aggravating factors and mitigating circumstances as directed by Florida Statute 921.141. The Court has also examined any other aspect of the Defendant's character, record, or any of the circumstances of the offense in compliance with court case 438 U.S. 586, 98 S.Ct. 2945, 57 L.Ed.2d 1973 (1978). The Court carefully considered the arguments both in favor of and in opposition to the death penalty, as well as all of the facts and evidence presented in the guilt and penalty phases of the trial and at the special hearing. Lastly, the Court has viewed and considered the credibility of every witness who testified in this matter.

Florida Statute 921.141 requires this Court to independently weigh the aggravating factors and mitigating circumstances presented in the Defendant's case and make written findings regarding the existence of those factors and circumstances, the sufficiency thereof and to assign them legal weight. If aggravating factors are proven beyond and to the exclusion of any reasonable doubt, the I spe#cer v. s,c,,e, 691 So.2d 5'862 (Fla.1996).

SENTENCING ORDER
STATE VS. LEO LANCING BOATMAN
CASE No. 04-2019-CF-000706-B
PAGE 3

Court must then examine any mitigating circumstances that have been proven by the greater weight of the evidence. If mitigating circumstances have been proven by the greater weight of the evidence, then the Court must determine if the aggravating factors outweigh the mitigating circumstances. The Court's findings must be in writing and be filed with the Clerk of the Court.

The Court has heard and considered the testimony

and the evidence presented during both the guilt phase proceeding and the penalty phase proceeding and finds as follows:

FACTS

On July 5, 2019, the Defendant, along with his co-defendant, William E. Wells, entered the dayroom in I-Wing in Florida State Prison with the premeditated intent to kill the victim, William Chapman. Florida State Prison is a maximum-security prison. And, at the time of the murder, the Defendant was serving two life sentences for first-degree murders which he committed in Marion County, Florida. Additionally, the Defendant was on close management (level 3) at the prison.

Upset that their close management level would not be reduced, the Defendant and Wells decided to kill a fellow inmate as an act of revenge against the Department of Corrections.

Ultimately, they chose inmate William Chapman as the intended victim because he had disrespected the Defendant on the prison wing. In preparation for the murder, the Defendant and Wells acquired shanks and ligatures to facilitate the killing. It appears that the Defendant acquired the shanks (metal rods) while Wells acquired the ligatures. The Defendant would not disclose from where he obtained the shanks.

SENTENCING ORDER
STATE VS. LEO LANCING BOATMAN
CASE No. 04-2019-CF-000706-B
PAGE 4

The events which occurred on July 5, 2019, were captured on video (both inside the dayroom and in the hallway outside the dayroom). The dayroom video reflects the Defendant, his co-defendant Wells, the victim, and approximately 10-12 other inmates in the dayroom before the attack began. The dayroom's singular door is the only entry and exit point into the room.

Approximately ten minutes before the attack began, the Defendant leaves the dayroom with a correctional officer to go to the bathroom; and he returns two minutes later. After the Defendant returns to the room, Wells leaves the room and is escorted to the bathroom. Once Wells returns to the room, the Defendant walks over to the victim, speaks to him, and the two walk out of the dayroom camera's view into an area that contains a blind spot. Wells then moves toward where the Defendant and Chapman are standing and wraps a white ligature around Chapman's neck. While Wells is strangling Chapman, the Defendant begins punching him.

Chapman can be seen struggling as the two co-defendants are choking and hitting him. The Defendant then moves in front of the dayroom door, blocking it with his foot. He then pulls out two large shanks, one in each hand, tied to his wrists. The Defendant tied the shanks to his wrists to prevent Chapman from taking them from him during the attack. During the attack, correctional officers unsuccessfully attempted to open the dayroom door, blocked by the Defendant with his body and foot. Further, the Defendant threatened the officers, telling them that he and Wells intended to kill Chapman ("This guy's going to die today"); and if they entered the dayroom they would be killed, or harmed, as well. As the attack continued, the Defendant and Wells stabbed Chapman in his eyes, neck, torso, back, and face. Although the correctional officers were ordering the Defendant to stop, the Defendant persisted in viciously attacking Chapman.

————————————————————

SENTENCING ORDER
STATE VS. LEO LANCING BOATMAN
CASE No. 04-2019-CF-000706-B
PAGE 5

At this point, correctional officers were able to slightly open the dayroom door and deploy a chemical agent into the room. Once the door was ajar, Chapman placed his fingers in the gap, trying to open the door and escape. However, Chapman was unable to get away from the Defendant and Wells' attack. Wells then began leaning against the dayroom door while the Defendant continued stabbing Chapman. The Defendant then gives Wells one of the shanks. Wells begins stabbing Chapman, ultimately leaving one of the shanks in the victim's neck. As he and Wells are stabbing Chapman, the Defendant continues to communicate with the correctional officers who were situated outside of the dayroom door. Ultimately, Chapman falls to the floor; and the Defendant and Wells take a short break. The Defendant can be seen on the dayroom video, covered in the victim's blood, appearing to revel in what he has done. The Defendant subsequently stomps on the victim seven times. After which, he stabs the victim with the second shank, leaving it in the back of his neck. The Defendant then stomps on the shank with such strength that it bends the metal. The entire attack lasted approximately 12 minutes.

Once the Defendant and Wells were certain that

Chapman was dead, they allowed the correctional officers into the room. Ultimately, Chapman was unable to be revived. And it was determined that his death was the result of being beaten, stabbed, and strangled. The medical examiner testified that Chapman had multiple traumas to his head, neck, eyes, face, and body, including: 25 stab wound/cuts on the right-side of his neck; 13 stab/cut wounds on the back of his neck; a penetrating injury to his neck by a metal rod (which was still in the victim's neck at the time of the autopsy); a deep ligature furrow in his neck (indicating that he had been strangled with a ligature); hemorrhaging around the eyes (the eyes themselves were intact); internal injuries (brain

————————————————————

SENTENCING ORDER
STATE VS. LEO LANCING BOATMAN
CASE No. 04-2019-CF-000706-B
PAGE 6

hemorrhaging caused by blunt force trauma; and multiple torso injuries (both internal and external) caused by penetrating injuries due to sharp force trauma. There were multiple modalities of injury and any of the more serious forms of blunt force trauma or sharp force trauma could have been the fatal act.

Hours after the murder, the Defendant was interviewed by FDLE Special Agents David Meachan and Garrett Carlisle. During the interview, the Defendant stated that he decided, after being required to stay on close management, that he was no longer going to put up with "the bullshit"; and that the next person who "crossed the line" would die. That person ended up being William Chapman. The Defendant felt betrayed by Chapman, whom he considered to be a friend.

According to the Defendant, Chapman was "an undercover fag" who was acting on behalf of another inmate to trick him and Wells into performing homosexual acts in exchange for coffee, and related items. The Defendant further acknowledged that he had been planning the murder for up to a week prior, but at least for a few days.

AGGRAVATING CIRCUMSTANCES

1. THE CAPITAL FELONY WAS COMMITTED BY A PERSON PREVIOUSLY CONVICTED OF A FELONY AND UNDER SENTENCE OF IMPRISONMENT. § 921.141(6)(a), FLA. STAT. (2019).

The Court finds that this aggravating circumstance has been proven beyond a reasonable doubt. The unrefuted testimony and evidence presented during the penalty phase proceeding established that the Defendant was under a sentence of imprisonment in the Florida Department of Corrections at the time of the murder. It is undisputed that, at the time of the murder, the Defendant was serving prison sentences for the following:

SENTENCING ORDER
STATE VS. LEO LANCING BOATMAN
CASE No. 04-2019-CF-000706-B
PAGE 7

(a) Marion County Case Number 42-2006-CF-000113-A:
　(i) First-Degree Murder with a Firearm (Life Imprisonment).

   (ii) First-Degree Murder with a Firearm (Life Imprisonment).

(b) Dixie County Case Number 15-2009-CF-000212-A:
   (i) Attempted Second-Degree Murder (7 years' imprisonment).

(c) Charlotte County Case Number 08-2011-CF-000061-A:
   (i) Third-Degree Murder (188 months' imprisonment).

Further, it is undisputed that the Defendant was serving these sentences at Florida State Prison, a maximum-security prison, at the time the murder occurred; and the Defendant was on close management. Thus, the Defendant did not merely commit the murder in this case while imprisoned. He committed the murder while under a heightened form of management at a maximum-security prison.

2. THE DEFENDANT WAS PREVIOUSLY CONVICTED OF ANOTHER CAPITAL FELONY OR OF A FELONY INVOLVING THE USE OR THREAT OF VIOLENCE TO THE PERSON. § 921.141(6)(b), FLA. STAT. (2019).

The Court finds that this aggravating circumstance has been proven beyond a reasonable doubt. "Qualitatively, [the] prior violent felony [aggravator is one of] the weightiest aggravators set out in the statutory sentencing scheme." Court case 55, So. 3d 515, 542 (Fla. 2010). As mentioned under the previous aggravator, the unrefuted testimony and evidence presented during the penalty phase trial established that the Defendant was under a sentence of two life sentences for two counts of first-degree murder; one count of attempted

SENTENCING ORDER
STATE VS. LEO LANCING BOATMAN
CASE No. 04-2019-CF-000706-B
PAGE 8

second-degree murder; and one count of third-degree murder. The Court notes that these convictions arose from three separate cases, two of which occurred while the Defendant was serving life sentences for first-degree murder. Both murder and attempted murder involve violence per se. Court case 442 So. 2d 193,197 (Fla.1983). Thus, the commission of these crimes inherently involves the threat of violence. Jd.

3. THE CAPITAL FELONY WAS ESPECIALLY HEINOUS, ATROCIOUS, OR CRUEL. § 921.141(6)(h), FLA. STAT. (2019).

The Court finds that this aggravating circumstance has been proven beyond a reasonable doubt. The heinous, atrocious, or cruel (HAC) aggravating factor applies in physically and mentally torturous murders which can be exemplified by the desire to inflict a high degree of pain or utter indifference to or enjoyment of the suffering of another. Court case 834 So. 2d 836, 849-50 (Fla. 2002) (citing court case 574 So.2d 136 (Fla.1991)). HAC focuses on the means and manner in which the death is inflicted and the immediate circumstances surrounding the death, rather than the intent and motivation of a defendant, where a victim experiences the torturous anxiety and fear of impending death. Jd. (citing court case 721 So.2d 274, 277 (Fla.1998); see court case 808 So. 2d 110, 134 (Fla. 2001)) ("For HAC to apply, the crime must be conscienceless or pitiless and unnecessarily torturous to the victim."). The HAC aggravator has been repeatedly upheld where, as here, the victim was repeatedly stabbed and remained conscious during and after the attack. Court case 859 So. 2d 465, 478 (Fla. 2003) (citing court case 808 So.2d at 134-35). The fear and emotional strain preceding the death may also be considered as contributing to the heinous nature of the

----

SENTENCING ORDER
STATE VS. LEO LANCING BOATMAN
CASE No. 04-2019-CF-000706-B
PAGE 9

crime. Jd.

The State introduced video evidence of the murder and testimony from the medical examiner establishing that the primary mechanism of death was multiple stabbings by metal shanks, blunt force trauma, and strangulation by use of a ligature. The medical examiner testified that Chapman had multiple traumas to his head, neck, eyes, face, and body, including: 25 stab wound/cuts on the right-side of his neck; 13 stab/cut wounds on the back of his neck; a penetrating injury to his neck by a metal rod (which was still in the victim's neck at the time of the autopsy); a deep ligature furrow in his neck (indicating that he had been strangled with a ligature); hemorrhaging around the eyes (the eyes themselves were intact); internal injuries (brain hemorrhaging) caused by blunt force trauma; and multiple torso injuries (both internal and external) caused by penetrating injuries due to sharp force trauma.

The video of the murder shows a torturous attack on the victim. For over 10 minutes the victim, William Chapman, is brutally beaten, stabbed, strangled, and stomped by the Defendant and his co-defendant William Wells while correctional officers and at least one other inmate (Reginald Arline), tell him to stop. During the attack, the victim pled for his life, and attempted to escape from the dayroom, without any respite.

The testimony and evidence show an attack that was intended not only to kill the victim but to make him suffer physically and mentally. The victim was aware that he was going to die; and that no help was coming for him. The level of fear and hopelessness that the victim was experiencing is clear from the testimony and evidence presented to this Court.

Further, the Defendant refused to allow correctional officers into the dayroom to help the

----

SENTENCING ORDER
STATE VS. LEO LANCING BOATMAN
CASE No. 04-2019-CF-000706-B
PAGE 10

victim, threatening to kill them as well if they intervened, thereby prolonging the victim's pain and suffering. Both during and after the merciless attack, the victim was faced with the reality that his death was imminent. And the Defendant was totally indifferent to the victim's suffering.

4. THE CAPITAL FELONY WAS A HOMICIDE AND WAS COMMITTED IN A COLD, CALCULATED, AND PREMEDITATED MANNER WITHOUT ANY PRETENSE OF MORAL OR LEGAL JUSTIFICATION. § 921.141(6)(i), FLA. STAT. (2019).

The Court finds that this aggravating circumstance has been proven beyond a reasonable doubt. For a cold, calculated, and premeditated (CCP) aggravator to be justified, it must meet a four-part test: (1) the killing must have been the product of cool and calm reflection and not an act prompted by emotional frenzy, panic, or a fit of rage (cold); (2) the defendant must have had a careful plan or prearranged design to commit murder before the fatal incident (calculated); (3) the defendant must have exhibited heightened premeditation (premeditated); and, (4) there must have been no pretense of moral or legal justification. Court case 841 So. 2d 362, 371 (Fla. 2003) (citing court case 800 So.2d 182,192 (Fla.2001)).

This aggravating circumstance pertains specifically to the state of mind, intent, and motivation of the defendant, and involves a much higher degree of premeditation than that required to prove first-degree murder. Brown v. S,a,e., 143 So. 3d 392, 402 (Fla. 2014) (citing court case 19 So.3d 277, 298 (Fla.2009); Court case 995 So.2d 351, 381-82 (Fla.2008)). To support a finding of CCP, the evidence must establish beyond a reasonable doubt that the defendant planned or prearranged to commit murder before the crime began. Jd. (citing court case 37 So.3d 187, 195 (Fla.2010)). The aggravating factor can be established by circumstances

---

SENTENCING ORDER
STATE VS. LEO LANCING BOATMAN
CASE No. 04-2019-CF-000706-B
PAGE 11

demonstrating advance procurement of a weapon, lack of resistance or provocation by the victim, and the appearance of a killing carried out as a matter of course.

Jd. (citing court case 965 So.2d 79, 98 (Fla.2007)).

The manner and circumstances of the crime demonstrate careful planning to ensure the desired result (the death of the victim) which is supported by the Defendant's own admissions to the FDLE special agents. While under close management in Florida State Prison, a maximum security prison, the Defendant was able to obtain the shanks used during the murder, prior to the date of the murder; the Defendant was able to hide the shanks outside of his cell in a location that he could easily access; the Defendant chose the intended victim at least three days prior to the murder; the Defendant planned the murder of the victim with another inmate (co-defendant William Wells) who was also on close management; and the Defendant planned with Wells for ligatures to be obtained and hidden by Wells in preparation for the murder. The Defendant used ligatures to tie the shanks to his wrists to prevent the shanks from being taken from him by the victim during the attack. The Defendant coordinated with his co-defendant for each of them to leave the dayroom in advance of the attack to obtain the shanks and ligatures. The Defendant planned, in advance, for the blocking of the dayroom door to prevent the entry of correctional officers and the escape of the victim. Given the level of oversight and supervision the Defendant was under leading up to and immediately prior to the murder, the Defendant could not have committed this murder, and coordinated it with fellow inmate William Wells, without significant, careful planning and deliberate forethought. The murder of William Chapman was not a decision that was made in the moment. And there is no credible evidence that Chapman was an actual threat

––––––––––––––––––––––

SENTENCING ORDER
STATE VS. LEO LANCING BOATMAN
CASE No. 04-2019-CF-000706-B
PAGE 12

to either the Defendant or Wells. Even the inmate (Smurf) whom Chapman worked for did nothing to intervene during the attack, despite being physically present in the dayroom at that time. The murder in this case was not the product of an actual fear or threat. It was the product, primarily, of an anger generated by the continuation of the Defendant on close management. The target of the murder was dictated and ultimately identified due to the Defendant feeling disrespected by Chapman.

Further, there is no credible evidence of a moral or legal justification for the murder. "[A] pretense of legal or moral justification is defined as any colorable claim based at least partly on uncontroverted and believable factual evidence or testimony that, but for its incompleteness, would constitute an excuse, justification, or defense as to the homicide." Court case 25 So. 3d 518, 534 (Fla. 2009) (quoting court case 991 So. 2d 364, 376-77 (Fla. 2008)). Here, even if the Court were to believe that the victim was "trying" the Defendant to the point that the Defendant felt he could be attacked by the victim, there is no credible evidence that the victim, who until a few days prior had been the Defendant's friend, had any intent to attack the Defendant. There is no credible evidence that the Defendant was under any actual threat prior to, or at the time of, the murder.

MITIGATING CIRCUMSTANCES

1. THE CAPITAL FELONY WAS COMMITTED WHILE THE DEFENDANT WAS UNDER THE INFLUENCE OF EXTREME MENTAL OR EMOTIONAL DISTURBANCE. § 921.141(7)(B), FLA. STAT. (2019).

This mitigating circumstance applies to defendants whose mental condition at the time of the murder was less than insanity but more

————————————————————

SENTENCING ORDER
STATE VS. LEO LANCING BOATMAN
CASE No. 04-2019-CF-000706-B
PAGE 13

than the emotions of an average man, which may have interfered with, but not obviated, his knowledge of right and wrong. Court case 441 So. 2d 606, 609 (Fla. 1983). A defendant may be legally answerable for his actions and legally sane, and even though he may be capable of assisting his counsel at trial, he may still deserve some mitigation of sentence because of his mental state. Id.

The Defendant's mental health history is well-documented; and extends back to his unstable childhood. He has been diagnosed with a variety of mental health disorders as well as neurocognitive brain damage. Dr. Joseph Wu, a neurologist, examined the Defendant's brain to determine his neurocognitive issues. Utilizing a Positron Emission Tomography (PET) scan, Dr. Wu determined that the Defendant suffers from neurocognitive brain abnormalities consistent with traumatic brain injury (TBI), fetal alcohol spectrum disorder (FASD), post-traumatic stress disorder (PTSD), and damage caused by adverse childhood experiences

(ACE's). The Defendant has cognitive defects related to the regulation of anger and impulse control. Dr. Michael Quinones, who examined the Defendant's records from childhood and adolescence, attributes the Defendant's cognitive defects to his voluminous number of ACE's, which are all well-documented and not in dispute.

As a child, the Defendant experienced physical, emotional, and sexual abuse and neglect in the home of his maternal grandmother, Ethel Lucille Boatman. Lucille Boatman (whom some in her family called "Lucifer") lorded over a home environment that was chaotic, hostile, Dr. Geoffrey Colino also testified regarding the Defendant's fetal alcohol spectrum disorder.

SENTENCING ORDER
STATE VS. LEO LANCING BOATMAN
CASE No. 04-2019-CF-000706-B
PAGE 14

inconsistent, and traumatizing. This environment was rife with family members with mental illness who were substance abusers. The Defendant had a mother who was absent for most of his life; who conceived him with an unknown father in a psychiatric hospital; who birthed him in that same psychiatric hospital; and who passed away while the Defendant was still young and impressionable under suspicious circumstances. The Defendant's negative home environment was only exacerbated as he entered foster care.

The Defendant had difficulty in school, both academically and behaviorally, which ultimately led to him entering the juvenile justice system. The Defendant spent most of his adolescence in confinement in juvenile detention facilities.

It is undisputed that the Defendant's childhood experiences profoundly affected his brain development and led to his impulsivity and criminality as an adolescent. The Defendant increasingly presented aggressive behavior to the world around him as he aged towards adulthood.

The Defendant lacked consistent caregiving and emotional support, which ultimately led to him moving from being a juvenile delinquent to an adult criminal.

It is also undisputed that the Defendant was under the stress of being denied release from close management and his belief that he would be on close management indefinitely. The Defendant felt hopeless about his situation.

Yet, despite these experiences, and the opinion of the experts who testified in mitigation, there is no credible evidence that the Defendant was under the influence of extreme mental or emotional disturbance at the time of the murder of William Chapman. The evidence in this case speaks to the contrary. The evidence shows a calculated, well-planned, coordinated attack on the

––––––––––––––––––––––––

SENTENCING ORDER
STATE VS. LEO LANCING BOATMAN
CASE No. 04-2019-CF-000706-B
PAGE 15

victim; and an admitted intent to seek retribution against the Department of Corrections for denying him release from close management. There is no credible evidence that the Defendant was unaware of his actions in the dayroom; or that he was caught up in the moment of an emotional reaction. In fact, the Defendant engaged with the correctional officers and other inmates calmly, coolly, and collectedly prior to the murder. And during the murder, he was acutely aware of the need to block the door to prevent the officers' entry; and the need to coordinate the stabbing, beating, and strangling with his co-defendant. The Defendant was clear-headed and goal-oriented in the days and minutes leading up to the murder, as well as during it.

2. THE VICTIM WAS A PARTICIPANT IN THE DEFENDANT'S CONDUCT OR CONSENTED TO THE ACT. § 921.141(7)(C), FLA. STAT. (2019).

There is no credible evidence that the victim threatened the Defendant either prior to or at the time of the murder. The victim had no knowledge that the attack was to take place. And once it began, the victim begged for his life and struggled to open the door for help until he was rendered unable to resist due to the wounds suffered.

3. THE DEFENDANT ACTED UNDER EXTREME DURESS OR UNDER THE SUBSTANTIAL DOMINATION OF ANOTHER PERSON. § 921.141(7)(E), FLA. STAT. (2019).

This mitigator was not established by the evidence. The evidence of the Defendant's substantial participation and planning in the murder has been discussed at length. The Defendant was an equal participant in the planning and execution of the victim in this case along with his co-defendant William Wells. Further, there is no credible evidence that the Defendant was under

SENTENCING ORDER
STATE VS. LEO LANCING BOATMAN
CASE No. 04-2019-CF-000706-B
PAGE 16

substantial domination of any person at the time of the planning and execution of the murder. And the Defendant's belief that he would never be released from close management does not constitute duress.

4. THE CAPACITY OF THE DEFENDANT TO APPRECIATE THE CRIMINALITY OF HIS CONDUCT OR TO CONFORM HIS CONDUCT TO THE REQUIREMENTS OF LAW WAS SUBSTANTIALLY IMPAIRED. § 921.141(7)(F), FLA. STAT. (2019).

"[C]ompetent, substantial evidence supports the rejection of expert testimony in support of the substantially impaired capacity mitigator where other evidence concerning the defendant's capacity conflicts with the expert testimony."

Court case 88 So. 3d 113, 124 (Fla. 2012). Further, "[e]vidence of 'logical steps' conflicts with expert testimony on this mitigator because they constitute 'purposeful actions' ... indicative of someone who knew those acts were wrong and who could conform his conduct to the law if he so desired." Jd. (quoting court case 965 So.2d 1,18 (Fla. 2007)).

Here, there is no credible evidence that the Defendant did not have the capacity to appreciate the criminality of his conduct or conform his conduct to the requirements of law. The Defendant fully understood the criminality of his actions leading up to, during, and after the murder. There is no credible evidence in this case that the Defendant's ability to conform his conduct was impaired or that he did not know that killing the victim was wrong. Court case 563 So. 2d 77, 80 (Fla.1990). Although the Defendant has an extensive mental health history, there is no evidence that he was not thinking clearly before, during, or immediately after his offense. Further, the record reflects that the Defendant was consistently a rational, cooperative,

---

SENTENCING ORDER
STATE VS. LEO LANCING BOATMAN
CASE No. 04-2019-CF-000706-B
PAGE 17

social, and well-behaved inmate in the years leading up to the murder. There is no credible evidence that the Defendant was manifesting abnormal mental health symptoms to the extent that he was a danger to himself or others prior to or after the murder; or any credible evidence that the Defendant did not appreciate what he was doing when the murder occurred. The Defendant admitted to the FDLE special agents that he planned and executed the murder with the purpose that it succeed without interruption. The Defendant's plan and execution of the murder belies any suggestion that he was unaware of the criminality and consequences of his actions.

5. THE AGE OF THE DEFENDANT AT THE TIME OF THE CRIME. § 921.141(7)(a), FLA. STAT. (2019).

The Court finds this mitigator was proven by the greater weight of the evidence and gives it some weight. "In Florida, numerical age alone may not be mitigating if not linked to some other material characteristic (e.g., immaturity)." Court case 136 So. 3d 1 125,1164 (Fla. 2014) (quoting court case 982 So.2d 649, 660 (Fla. 2008)). "Where a defendant is not a minor, no per se rule exists which pinpoints a particular age as an automatic factor in mitigation." Jd. (quoting court case 770 So.2d 1119,1133 (Fla. 2000)). "Instead, the trial judge must evaluate this mitigator based on the evidence adduced at trial and at the sentencing hearing." Id. Here, the Defendant was 32 years old at the time of the murder. And the sophistication and intelligence required for the Defendant, an inmate on close management at a maximum-security prison, to plan, coordinate, and execute the murder of the victim with another close management inmate reflects that the Defendant's age is not a mitigating factor in this case. The Defendant's actions and justifications reflect those of a person exhibiting age-appropriate behavior; and

---

SENTENCING ORDER
STATE VS. LEO LANCING BOATMAN
CASE No. 04-2019-CF-000706-B
PAGE 18

knowledge acquired over years of incarceration. The Defendant's planning and execution of the murder were sophisticated and rational.

6. THE EXISTENCE OF ANY OTHER FACTORS IN THE DEFENDANT'S BACKGROUND THAT WOULD MITIGATE AGAINST IMPOSITION OF THE DEATH PENALTY. § 921.141(7)(H), FLA. STAT. (2019).

NON-STATUTORY MITIGATING CIRCUMSTANCES

A. COURTROOM BEHAVIOR

The Court finds that this mitigator was proven by the greater weight of the evidence and gives it some weight. The Defendant has consistently exhibited absolute respect for the process and for everyone involved in this case: the Court, the State Attorney's office, the court personnel, the Clerk of Court's staff, the correctional officers who transported him, and his defense team. He has always been polite and courteous, even when under the tremendous, and undeniable, stress of a trial and a penalty phase proceeding.

B. WAIVED JURY

The Court finds that this mitigator was proven by the greater weight of the evidence and gives it some weight. The fact that the Defendant waived the jury during the penalty phase is indicative of his trust in the judicial system and his respect for the court. Further, the Defendant has expressed his belief that a jury should not be burdened with the decision of whether to sentence him to life or death. This explanation by the Defendant reflects his maturity and his understanding of the seriousness of this proceeding. Throughout the penalty phase of his trial, the Defendant has shown an appreciation of the jury system and the role of the Court in determining the appropriate sentence. The Defendant's sincere interest in protecting the jury from having to make a difficult

---

SENTENCING ORDER
STATE VS. LEO LANCING BOATMAN
CASE No. 04-2019-CF-000706-B
PAGE 19

decision is mitigating; however, when weighed against the facts and evidence of this case it deserves only limited weight.

C. CARE FOR THE COMMUNITY AND FAMILY

The Court finds that this mitigator was proven by the greater weight of the evidence and gives it some weight. The undisputed testimony and evidence presented by the Defendant's family and friends reflects a person who genuinely cares for those who are close to, and supportive of, him. And there is overwhelming evidence that the Defendant is loved and valued by his family and friends, including fellow inmates. The Defendant was known among his fellow inmates as someone who was generous and gregarious. And his family and friends see past his actions in this case to a person that is genuine and principled in his daily life. Yet, the court notes the Defendant considered the victim in this case a close friend until he mercilessly beat, stabbed, and stomped him to death in front of other inmates and correctional officers. Although the Defendant felt betrayed by the victim, as fellow inmate Reginald Arline noted in his testimony, the victim's disrespect was universal towards all the inmates on the wing and not directed especially at the Defendant. Any "betrayal" of their friendship by the victim was outweighed by the Defendant's betrayal of their friendship by his brutal murder of the victim.

D. GENERATIONAL TRAUMA

The Court finds that this mitigator was proven by the greater weight of the evidence and gives it some weight. The undisputed testimony and evidence presented by the Defendant's family and friends reflects the existence of generational trauma in his family and the environment that he grew up in as a child. The Defendant was failed by his family, by the Department of Children and

———————————————————————

SENTENCING ORDER
STATE VS. LEO LANCING BOATMAN
CASE No. 04-2019-CF-000706-B
PAGE 20

Families, and by the Department of Juvenile Justice, all of whom were aware of the environment he came out of but who were either unwilling or unable to stop the generational trauma from being passed on to the Defendant. The Defendant's letters to former Judge Irene Sullivan communicate the Defendant's awareness of this trauma; and how it formed the child who would become the man that he is today. It is clear to the Court that the Defendant did not become the person he is today in a vacuum. He was the product of profound generational dysfunction and abuse.

E. BRAIN MALFORMATION

The Court finds that this mitigator was proven by the greater weight of the evidence and gives it some weight. The undisputed testimony and evidence presented in this case reflects that the Defendant has brain abnormalities and cognitive deficits. Yet, the Defendant's childhood, adolescence, and adulthood indicate that the Defendant has always been, and continues to be, highly intelligent, perceptive, and social. The Defendant had friends as a child, with whom he exhibited no indicia of violence or criminality. The Defendant held jobs; was accepted at and attended some community colleges; and lived with his uncle, Victor Boatman, for a brief period in his late adolescence. And the Defendant has consistently exhibited in his life a level of sophistication that belies any suggestion that he struggles with his abnormalities and cognitive deficits. This Court has had substantial interaction with the Defendant in court. The Defendant is polite, respectful, and engaged. This Court's observations of the Defendant's high-functioning nature are consistent with those of his friends and family who testified. Any limitations that the Defendant has are not reflected in his ability to plan, communicate, and articulate his thoughts and ideas. The record reflects the Defendant's rationality, both prior to the murder and throughout the

————————————————————

SENTENCING ORDER
STATE VS. LEO LANCING BOATMAN
CASE No. 04-2019-CF-000706-B
PAGE 21

course of this case.

F. CONCEPTION (OR PERCEPTION OF CONCEPTION)

The Court finds that this mitigator was proven by the greater weight of the evidence and gives it some weight. The undisputed testimony and evidence presented in this case reflects that the Defendant was the product of the impregnation of his mother by an unknown male while she was a patient at a psychiatric facility. The circumstances of the Defendant's conception certainly had a profound impact on his life and emotional development.

G. FETAL ALCOHOL SYNDROME

The Court finds that this mitigator was proven by the greater weight of the evidence and gives it some weight. The undisputed testimony and evidence presented in this case reflects that the Defendant has fetal alcohol spectrum disorder. And that it affected the Defendant's childhood and adolescent development. The Defendant's mental health, difficulties with impulse control throughout his life, criminality, and poor judgment are certainly a product of this condition.

However, as previously discussed, the Defendant's demonstrable intelligence, ability to plan, communication skills (both orally and in writing), and overall respectful and social demeanor do not support the premise that he struggles with this disorder. Rather, aside from the defense experts' conclusory opinions, the record indicates that the Defendant has exceptional insight and capacity to avoid conflict when he chooses to do so. Further, the Defendant has no difficulty making and maintaining friendships; following directions and orders; or coordinating with others when he chooses to do so.

H. INSTABILITY IN THE HOME

––––––––––––––––––––––––––

SENTENCING ORDER
STATE VS. LEO LANCING BOATMAN
CASE No. 04-2019-CF-000706-B
PAGE 22

The Court finds that this mitigator was proven by the greater weight of the evidence and gives it some weight. The undisputed testimony and evidence presented in this case reflects that the Defendant was the product of an unstable home environment. The Defendant bounced around his family, ultimately ending up in a foster home that was equally abusive and neglectful. The lack of control that the Defendant felt contributed to his poor decision-making and criminality as a juvenile, and ultimately as an adult. The Defendant's issues with lack of trust of others and the systems that have controlled his life are certainly connected to the instability of his youth.

I. JUVENILE COMMITMENT FROM AGE 14

The Court finds that this mitigator was proven by the greater weight of the evidence and gives it some weight. The undisputed testimony and evidence presented in this case reflects that the Defendant was in confinement in juvenile detention facilities throughout his adolescence.

During this time, the Defendant experienced solitary confinement and was conditioned into becoming the incarcerated individual that he is today. The Defendant was failed by the Department of Children and Families and by the Department of Juvenile Justice, both of which allowed him to become a career criminal early in his life. And the Defendant was certainly impacted by his experiences of being incarcerated as a youth, which only exacerbated the other mitigating factors addressed in this order.

J. SEXUAL ABUSE

The Court finds that this mitigator was proven by the greater weight of the evidence and gives it some weight. The undisputed testimony and evidence presented in this case reflects that the Defendant was sexually abused by numerous individuals throughout his childhood and

————————————————————

SENTENCING ORDER
STATE VS. LEO LANCING BOATMAN
CASE No. 04-2019-CF-000706-B
PAGE 23

adolescence. Although the Defendant's experience of being sexually abused as a child certainly affected him, there is no credible evidence that it has impacted him as an adult. The record reflects that the Defendant has maintained positive relationships with inmates who are both homosexual and transgender. And there is no evidence that the Defendant harbors any animosity against any inmates who do not seek to take advantage of him sexually or disrespect his disinterest in homosexual activity. The Defendant does not seem traumatized by his sexual abuse in his youth.

And there is no credible evidence that his experiences with sexual abuse as a child directly impacted his life in prison as an adult.

K. ADVERSE CHILDHOOD EXPERIENCES (ACE's)

The Court finds that this mitigator was proven by the greater weight of the evidence and gives it some weight. The undisputed testimony and evidence presented in this case reflects that the Defendant has 8 out of 10 ACE's. The Defendant's exposure to these ACE's certainly profoundly impacted his physical, emotional, and social development; and undermined any chance that he had to succeed in life in a non-incarcerative environment. Further, there is credible evidence that the Defendant's ACE's exacerbated his fetal alcohol spectrum disorder and mental illness.

However, the Defendant's ACE's and other

mitigators addressed in this order overlap. This Court has considered the Defendant's ACE's throughout. And although this Court gives them weight, both individually and cumulatively, they must be considered in light of the Defendant's positive experiences as a juvenile. The Defendant was not unloved or uncared for. The Defendant had some supportive family members and persons in his life who encouraged him; and who gave him opportunities to work outside the home and engage in extracurricular activities. Although the cumulative nature of the Defendant's ACE's is stunning, the record reflects that the Defendant

— —

SENTENCING ORDER
STATE VS. LEO LANCING BOATMAN
CASE No. 04-2019-CF-000706-B
PAGE 24

built lasting relationships during his childhood and adolescence. The Defendant's early life, though difficult, was not without hope, love, and opportunity.

L. MERCY

The Court finds that this mitigator was proven by the greater weight of the evidence and gives it little weight. Regardless of the results of the weighing process, even if the court finds that the sufficient aggravators outweigh the mitigators, the law neither compels nor requires it to determine that the Defendant should be sentenced to death. See Fla. Std. Jury Instr. (Crim.) 7.11.

Throughout the Court's weighing process, it has considered the notion of mercy in determining the appropriate sentence in this case.

CONCLUSION

The Court understands that the process of weighing the aggravating and mitigating circumstances is not simply a mathematical process. It is more qualitative than quantitative. In that regard, the Court finds that the aggravating circumstances in this case far outweigh the mitigating circumstances. And, in considering the mitigating circumstances presented by the Defendant, this Court has considered them within their respective categories. Although specific mitigating circumstances addressed in the Defendant's sentencing memorandum may not have been particularly articulated above, this court has considered them contextually within the categories listed above; and given them the appropriate weight as part of those substantive categories.

The Defendant has an extensive history of violent felony offenses; and, at the time of the murder in this case, was serving two life sentences in the Florida Department of Corrections based

—————————————————————————

SENTENCING ORDER
STATE VS. LEO LANCING BOATMAN
CASE No. 04-2019-CF-000706-B
PAGE 25

on three separate and distinct criminal episodes involving violence or threats of violence. In this case, the Defendant planned, in a cold, calculated, and premeditated manner, the murder of the victim for days before he committed it. The Defendant obtained shanks prior to the murder; and hid them in an easily accessible location outside of his cell. Further, the Defendant coordinated with his co-defendant to make ligatures with which to tie the shanks to his wrists; and by which his co-defendant could strangle the victim. Without any pretense of legal or moral justification, the Defendant brutally stabbed the victim multiple times, during which the victim pled for his life knowing that death was imminent. The Defendant stomped the victim and stabbed him in the eyes; and encouraged his co-defendant to mercilessly stab the victim. The murder in this case was carried out as a matter of course, without any threat from the victim. And while carrying it out openly in front of other inmates as well as correctional officers, the Defendant took actions, and made threats, to ensure that no one would intervene until the murder was completed to his satisfaction.

These aggravating circumstances far outweigh the mitigating circumstances which the Court has heard and considered. Furthermore, this Court finds that any of the considered aggravating factors found in this case, standing alone, would be sufficient to outweigh the total weight of all the mitigation presented regarding the murder of William Chapman.

JUDGMENT AND SENTENCE

As to the Charge of First-Degree Murder of William L. Chapman in the Indictment, the Court adjudicates you, LEO L. BOATMAN, guilty of that offense and sentences you to death.

IT IS ORDERED that you, LEO L. BOATMAN, be taken by the proper authority to the

————————————————————————

SENTENCING ORDER
STATE VS. LEO LANCING BOATMAN
CASE No. 04-2019-CF-000706-B
PAGE 26

Florida Department of Corrections, to be housed there until the date of your execution, IT IS FURTHER ORDERED that on such scheduled date, you, LEO L. BOATMAN, be put to death.

You are hereby notified that this Sentence is subject to automatic review by the Florida Supreme Court.

DONE AND ORDERED in Chambers at Starke, Bradford County, Florida, on this 9th day of November 2022.

JAMES M. COLAW,

CIRCUIT JUDGE

CERTIFICATE OF SERVICE

I CERTIFY that a true copy of the foregoing was furnished by e-mail delivery on this 9th day of November 2022 to:

Kristofer Eisenmenger, Asst. Public Defender

Public Defender's Office

151 SW 2nd Ave,

Gainesville, FL 32601

eisermen do8.or

eservice@,ndo 8. org

Luis Bustanante, Asst. State Attorney

State Attorney's Office

945 N. Temple Ave,

Starke, Florida, 32091

Chapter 31

Death Row Amenities
Dewey Caruthers

Leo allegedly committed his fourth murder in large part to get sent to death row, which offers better living conditions than Florida's maximum security or close management.

Leo's many stints as a juvenile in solitary confinement for days and weeks at a time made the isolation of maximum security and close management pure suffering. But there was hope for better accommodations by murdering someone in a premeditated manner—the endgame a transfer to death row. This seems to be what motivated Boatman and fellow inmate William Wells to murder inmate William Chapman, who was due to be released in six months.

This is strikingly similar to the case of James Robertson, a death row inmate in a Florida prison whose story was in the acclaimed Netflix documentary *I Am a Killer* series. Robertson wanted out of the isolated environment of maximum security and into the better digs of death row.

"I knew they was going to use any excuse they could to keep me (in solitary confinement)," Robertson said in the documentary. "Any excuse. Finally, I got mad and I said, 'I'ma go ahead and kill somebody.' Believe me, it was premeditated, all the way," he added. In the documentary, Robertson and his nurse, Ann Attwell, openly talk about the better conditions for death row inmates. She explained the difference between death row and close management as "the difference between the slums and Beverly Hills."

"On death row, Robertson had his own television, his own bedspread, better food, an individual nurse to take care of him, and a generally more quiet atmosphere."

Ann Atwell, Florida State Prison death row nurse

Amenity #1: Personal TV and radio

Inmates in general population have access to televisions in the common living spaces. Prisoners in maximum security and close management, usually there for additional punishment, often get no TV privileges. However, in Florida death row inmates have personal televisions and radios.

Amenity #2: Personal bedding

Bedding for prisoners in maximum security and close management is similar to a hotel in that it shares bedding randomly among guests or inmates. But death row inmates are allowed to have their own bedspread, a valuable personal possession.

Amenity #3: Better food

The personal meals for death row inmates are considered better than the food offered in maximum security, close management or general population.

Amenity #4: Personal nurse

Maximum security and close management prisoners, like those in general population, see various nurses for health issues and check-ups. Death row inmates in Florida, however, have personal nurses to take care of them.

Amenity #5: Quiet atmosphere

General population, maximum security and close management can get loud—at times, it's constant yelling and screaming for hours. However, death row offers a quieter atmosphere. "Death row you can hear a pin drop," Atwell said.

"In close management we deal with a lot of frustration," Atwell said. "They sleep most of the day, but if you go by at night...they're fighting with one another. You can hear them, all night long."

Amenity #6: Safety and camaraderie

General population can be dangerous and in some instances is fatal. As an example, Boatman allegedly co-murdered his last victim in a waiting room full of at least a dozen inmates with a guard down the hall—all under video surveillance.

Death row rarely has incidents of inmate-on-inmate violence, much less murder. Atwell explains death row inmates feel a camaraderie for each other. "They have this camaraderie that they're all there together," she said.

Also, many perceive themselves being sentenced to death row as a matriculation to the highest level of their criminal careers. "For them it's a safe haven," Atwell said, noting "they love death row."

Chapter 32

Five Solutions
Dewey Caruthers

Author's Note: Dewey Caruthers has vast expertise in the areas of foster care and juvenile justice. My experience as a juvenile judge leads me to adopt his five solutions in their entirety.

What can be done to prevent more Leo Boatmans? These five solutions will slow down the creation of violent, career criminals being produced in factories better known as the child welfare and juvenile justice systems.

1. Professional Foster Parents
2. Prearrest diversion civil citations
3. Restorative Justice
4. Credible Messengers
5. Rehabilitation over Punishment

Ninety percent of youth with five or more foster care placements will enter the justice system. It's called the foster care-to-prison pipeline.

Solution 1:

Professional foster parents are college-educated and trained to foster children as their full-time jobs, which provide middle-income wages.

The problem: Foster children are not at the top of the priority list in an irrefutably broken system.

What if the foster care system didn't just work but worked very well? What if we could take children upon initial traumatization from unsafe situations and place them in stable, functional middle-income homes where they would gain the love, support, attention and social skills needed to become successful adults with post-secondary educations? This ideal cannot be achieved with the current approach that places the foster care system and family reunification as higher priorities than foster children.

The solution: Make foster parenting a profession. If foster children were first and foremost, foster parenting would be a profession, giving the most challenged kids the best homes possible. Professional foster parents are college-educated and trained to foster children as their full-time careers, which provide middle-income wages.

Imagine Leo Boatman being sent to professional foster parents at age four, when the oversight agency first learned of sexual abuse. Instead of prioritizing family reunification, Boatman's interests would come first, placing him in a stable, middle-income foster family through high school. His life would have been completely different, with little chance that he would have become the monster that murdered two college students in the Ocala National Forest.

In 2008, more than 2 million youth were arrested in the United States, 95% of whom were not accused of a serious felony. Professional foster parents could have prevented many, many of them from future more serious crimes against property and people.

Furthermore, juvenile offenders have a very low rate of completing high school, which severely limits the types of jobs these prior offenders can get and leads them back into the prison cycle.

Solution 2:

Prearrest diversion civil citations keep youth out of a system that manufactures career criminals.

The problem: Tough-on-crime approaches to common youth misbehavior funnel kids into the school-to-prison pipeline.

Minor offenses like a fight with no injuries, stealing a $15 T-shirt, underage drinking and possession of marijuana—in previous days considered common youth misbehavior better handled by a parent or principal—are criminal offenses that anchor a child with a misdemeanor arrest record. For many students, an initial arrest for common youth misbehavior leads to another one, which in turn prompts the first of many felonies to come. Essentially, system involvement leads to greater system involvement—it's called the school-to-prison pipeline (and it is where most career criminals originate).

The solution: Keep kids out of the system, and from matriculating into career criminals, with prearrest diversion civil citations, which Florida has done successfully. Youth offenders take responsibility for their actions and are able to move forward without an arrest record. Children issued prearrest diversions have substantially lower recidivism rates than those arrested. A key component of success is the behavioral assessment to determine if the incident was a first-time, one-time offense or if there is risk of re-offending. If risk is detected, mental health services are mandated, such as anger management for fighting.

Boatman's first outburst in elementary school would have resulted in a prearrest diversion, triggering a family mental health assessment. He would have been removed from his grandmother, placed into a stable foster home, and given mental health treatment—all of which would have been a new direction that would have precluded Boatman from becoming a serial killer.

Solution 3:

Restorative justice brings real accountability to youth offenders, who are required to make amends with the victim.

The problem: Youth offenders are not required to make amends with the victim.

If repeat offenders learned their lessons from being arrested, they wouldn't be repeat offenders. Fueling the arrest cycle, some youth see arrests as incentives that escalate social status, such as how wearing an ankle monitor increases street credibility. Youth within the cycle don't learn the consequences of their negative actions on others.

The solution: Restorative justice requires young people to take personal responsibility for their actions and to repair the harm to victims. Making amends is vital during adolescent and teen years to understand right and wrong at later ages. Most importantly, restorative justice has much lower recidivism rates than the traditional juvenile legal system.

For Leo, restorative justice could have instilled at least a small amount of empathy—something he lacked completely when shooting two college students in the Ocala National Forest.

Two-thirds of youth who have been arrested will become repeat offenders within 24 months.

Solution 4:

Credible messengers are men and women, previously justice system-involved as youth, who engage repeat youth offenders in a peer-to-peer dynamic.

The problem: Repeat youth offenders don't listen to cops.

As research on kids who commit felonies shows, repeat youth offenders are not inclined to take a message from law enforcement about the short- and long-term dangers of criminal behavior. In many situations, cops lecturing these kids can actually be counterproductive.

The solution: The use of credible messengers is a proven public health strategy that is being adapted for use in criminal justice. If a person who has been through similar challenges delivers the message, juveniles are more likely to consider it.

Leo did not even have access to a probation officer, much less a credible messenger, as he continued to escalate his illegal behavior. Surely a credible messenger would have identified the widespread sexual and physical abuse of Leo, placing him into a safe home and immersing him in mental health treatments.

Confinement in youth corrections facilities doesn't work well as a strategy to steer delinquent youth away from crime as adults, as evidenced by re-arrest rates of 70% to 80% within two to three years.

Solution 5:

Shift the priorities of juvenile prison, focusing on rehabilitation over punishment.

The problem: Juvenile prisons transform potentially bad kids into violent career criminals.

When youth are released from the juvenile justice system in worse shape—more traumatized, more angry—than when they arrived, it should come as no surprise when they wreak violence on innocent people. This is the consequence, in large part, of the juvenile justice system prioritizing punishment over rehabilitation.

The solution: Juvenile detention centers, commitment programs and prisons should shift their priorities, focusing instead on rehabilitation over punishment. At some point, every single child in the juvenile justice system will be released. The question becomes: What kind of youth do we want re-entering our society—one who has been mostly punished or one mostly rehabilitated?

Boatman re-entered society as a young man who had been not just punished but harshly punished for his crimes, never receiving rehabilitation resources for the constant trauma throughout his childhood. If, upon entry to his first juvenile commitment program at age 13, Boatman had been greeted with mental health counseling instead of more sexual and physical abuse, would he still have murdered two college students at age 19, less than six months after leaving the system?

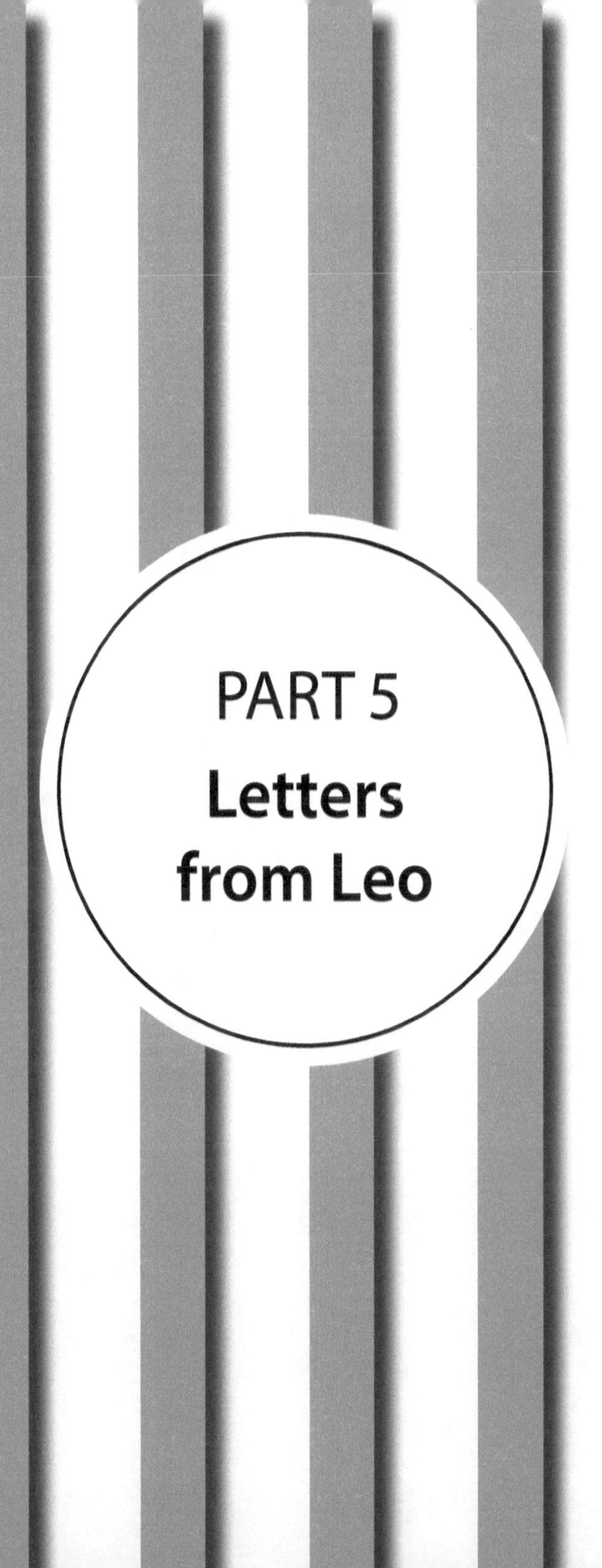

PART 5
Letters
from Leo

Daily Life in Prison

Dear Sullivan,

The Florida State Prison that I'm at today is much different than the one I stepped into for a short time in 2007. Back then, it was a lot more wild. But I've been here through four different wardens. Our latest is Warden Palmer, something of a problem fixer. I heard they send him to institutions to get them under control. Real strict.

Back in 2007 it was a mad house. You would go to rec and dudes would be having sex through the fences, fighting, stabbing each other. It's still a wild place, but nothing like back then.

As a CM, closed management, inmate, I'm in my cell all day, the whole twenty-four hours. The only time I come out is for three showers a week: Monday, Wednesday and Saturday. They cuff me up and lock me in a shower for about five to ten minutes.

My cell is pretty small. I've got a sink, toilet and bed plus a locker for my property. That takes up all my space. This prison has the smallest cells I've ever been in, smaller than other prisons, detention centers or jails.

I'm allowed rec three times a week, but it almost never happens. It is scheduled for one time on Monday, two times on Friday. Each time is for two hours outside in a cage next to hundreds of other cages. In order to go I have to get up before 6 a.m. and stand at the door to my cell until the officer makes the rec list. This could be at 6 a.m. or at times as late as 8 a.m. My room has to be perfect. I have to be clean shaven, nails clipped and butt naked when they get to my cell. Then I have to be strip searched, cuffed up and escorted to the cage.

All of this requires a lot of work for the officers. Even though rec is a right and not a privilege, they find reasons not to let you go. Sometimes they make it up, sometimes they just walk right past your cell like they don't even see you. So, fifty percent of the time you go through all the hoops to get on the rec list, and they don't let you go anyway. Lately they've started coming on unscheduled days now so that if you wanted to go, you would have to get up and go through all the BS every morning. As a result, I hardly ever go.

In my cell I have my books, magazines, letter writing material, some pictures, hygiene stuff, change of clothes, radio and sometimes a food item or two if I can order from the canteen once a week. You have to have money. They sell batteries for my radio there too.

My radio is the most important thing to closed management inmates. Some of the inmates don't even have that. All they can do is sit and stare at the walls all day. With a radio, you can follow sports, news, music and even the made for radio movies that come out on National Public Radio.

My days are almost always the same. I wake up at 5 a.m. when lights come on. I make my bed, wash my face, brush my teeth. By about 6:30 or 7:00 a.m. breakfast is slid through my tray flap. Then I normally go back to sleep until lunch, that comes around 11 a.m. After that I'll walk in circles in my cell for like an hour to get the blood flowing. Then I'll read if I have a book or listen to the radio for the rest of the day. Dinner comes at 6:30 p.m. The only high point in the week is Monday through Friday mail call. That comes between 7 and 10 p.m. We all wait and watch, hoping for a letter or magazine. If I get mail, I usually sit down right then and write back.

This is my schedule every day and I've been doing it forever, it seems.

We aren't really allowed to talk to inmates except for sign language out our windows. But we still manage to communicate. We play chess and talk about all kinds of stuff. Someone may have a good magazine for sale, so we make long lines out of sheets or threads out of our uniforms. Then we tie a heavy piece of soap on the line and slide it from cell to cell. A bunch of trading goes on.

Those who don't get money from home have to find a hustle if they want to eat snacks sometimes, get a radio or batteries, or have stuff to read. Some sell the food off their trays. Some gamble on sports, some draw pictures for family and friends or make cards.

The unofficial currency of it all is stamps. The trade has grown so much that there are even businesses that cater to inmates who can buy magazines with books of stamps. In the end, it all comes down to the ability to use the stamps to send mail in the hope that someone will write us back.

Permission to Improve Closed Management Level Denied

Dear Sullivan,

So much for the jury's verdict.

The jury in Charlotte County, Florida, found me not guilty of second-degree murder. Not "depraved," as the prosecutor said again and again, trying to convince the same jury to convict me of a heinous crime. Yes, they did find me guilty of a felony murder, as the guy died much later as a result of injuries from our fight, I guess. But it wasn't premeditated, it wasn't "depraved."

So my lawyers and I thought that verdict of a much lesser charge than the prosecutors wanted would help to get me off close management and into the general prison population, so that I could work some jobs, go to the library, sign up for some college courses and have more visitors. That's what we thought. I guess we were wrong.

There are three CM levels. I am currently on closed management two. I've been on that level for a year now. I was on closed management one for one year and before that on maximum management for two years, the most restrictive.

I haven't had any write ups, called disciplinary reports, since April of 2011. So I felt pretty good that at my next review I'd advance to the lowest closed management level. The jury's verdict plus the time elapsed since my last infraction clearly showed that I wasn't going to start any fights, or so I thought.

My wing officers said they would put in a good word for me, since as long as I've been on their wing, I've never made any trouble.

So, I had real good feelings when the guards took me to

the group inside the prison that makes these decisions every six months.

Only one other inmate had a hearing that week. The guards took us out, cuffed and put us in a holding cage to wait for the review board to assemble. When they came out on the wing, it was with a huge escort. It was the warden, assistant warden, head of classification and state classification employee, as well as the inmate's classification officer, sometimes the colonel, the major, a captain and four or five officers or guards who know the inmate.

These people take seats at tables and log on to computers to pull up the recommendations. When that was done, I was called up front and center. Ms. McLellan, who is head of classification, joked with me a little about how long I've been here, and then read the recommendation. Right away the warden and everyone agreed. Then they asked me if I had anything to say.

As you have guessed, the recommendation was not favorable. I was to stay on closed management two. So, when they asked, I told them how long I'd been on closed management and how long I've been discipline free, over three years. Also, the incident with the other prisoner was four years ago, and I was found guilty only of a lesser charge. I also said I was only asking for closed management three, not the compound, and that I still have a long way to go before I could join the open population.

It didn't matter. They said I was doing a good job, to keep at it, not get in any trouble and they would look at it again in six months.

I wanted to yell, "Fuck it all," but I held my temper. Truth is, I've been through way worse. Another six months won't kill me.

Six more months in this cell. Do they have any idea how long that is?

Executions, Guards and Interactions with Guards

Dear Sullivan,

You and others ask about executions. As if I would know more than you do, who get newspapers, watch TV, use the Internet, etc.

Well, here's the little I know, all from the inside.

Florida State Prison is the only prison in the state that holds executions. For the prisoners, like me, it's just like any other day, only shorter. The only way we know an execution is about to take place is that the guards or officers wear long sleeve shirts and ties. They feed you a few hours early. Then they lock the whole prison down around four p.m. They expect absolute quiet from that moment on, and they walk around in a bunch to make sure that inmates aren't yelling at the windows and what not.

This reminds me to point out what may be obvious. There is no air conditioning here and in the hot Florida summer, which now lasts six months, it is so hot inside our cells, hotter than outside, that it must reach 100 degrees.

So, the executions don't really affect us except for locking everything down and feeding us early. After that, it is business as usual. We don't know who or why or anything about the prisoners who were executed. They lived apart from us on death row.

You asked about guards, and I told you I wasn't going to name names, as our outgoing mail is read by them, and if they don't like what I say, you'll probably never get this letter.

If you think about it, although I'm only twenty-eight years old, I've experienced a lot of guards in confinement. I had them at the juvenile detention center, in some residential programs, at Omega Juvenile Prison, at Marion County Jail, Charlotte County Prison and then at Florida State Prison, where I am now. That's from age ten to age twenty-eight. Eighteen years of guards. So I guess I know something about them.

Just like people everywhere you get good guards and bad guards. To me, a good guard does his job and leaves you alone unless he is required by his job to do otherwise. Then you get some wise guys who get off on busting our chops. They go out of their way to find reasons to mess with us. Shake down every single day, sweat the small things like a magazine without your name on it, that kind of stuff.

You asked me about "interaction with the guards." It is nothing like juvenile facilities. You don't "interact" with the guards. The less you talk, the better. You don't want to be seen talking to the "police." It's a good way to get labeled as a snitch or to get hurt.

For instance, I talked to the police today, a friendly conversation. Then they had a shake down and got a cell phone off a dude. Everyone will think that I told, and that's my ass. So you basically avoid guards and police. They feed you, pass out mail, escort you, and that's it. Anything else is unusual. I'm in my cell all day and every thirty minutes they walk by.

That's all. We don't talk.

Dreams and
What Might Have Been

Dear Sullivan,

First of all, thanks for the stamps. I wish I had some way to repay you. You have no idea how much they help.

You keep writing to ask me what I see in my future, how I'm coping with my sentence. Don't you realize that I don't like to think about it? Especially right now, I'm in a rough slump and just scratching around.

The easiest way to think about my sentence is just to deny it. I don't deny that I got life, but I don't accept that I will die in prison. If I did, I would have nothing left to dream about, no future to look forward to. My dreams, daydreams, fantasies, are really all that sustains me. So I continue to think that maybe, somehow, some way, I'll get another chance at life.

In my heart I know I don't deserve it, but it is human nature to fight on. I made a horrible decision and realize that I deserve punishment. But I'm human too, and no one wants to be tormented the rest of their lives.

But when I think of what I would do if I ever got out, I am stumped. I still kind of want to just disappear into the wilderness. Another daydream is to get a decent sailboat and spend my days sailing to different countries and islands, enjoying the different cultures and geography. I think that I would have made a great anthropologist.

The Florida Department of Corrections is really corrupt. It's a bad system that has gotten worse. One of my personal goals is to try and get an interstate compact transfer to Colorado. I have several aunts and cousins there and Vic is going to be living there next year. Since he wasn't incarcerated in Colorado, he would be able to visit me. He can't do that here in Florida.

Plus, I'd be able to get a job. Hey, I might only make $1.50 a day, but it's better than nothing. Florida doesn't pay inmates to work. But if you are in the open population, it's mandatory that you work. Private medical or kitchen companies get free labor and make a huge profit.

There are so many more programs for inmates in other states. Plus, no one would know who I am, so it would be a fresh start and much easier to stay out of trouble.

System Improvements

Dear Sullivan,

I almost laughed out loud when I got your letter asking what changes I would make if I were head of the Department of Corrections, the Department of Juvenile Justice and the Department of Children and Families. Hah! It reminded me that I have been in all three of those systems since I was a toddler.

I think the biggest problem with all three systems is oversight. No one is really monitoring the situation at all. As a result there is no one to blow the whistle or cry foul.

Here in prison, there are plenty of groups who are supposed to do "inspections," but it's all a sham. They may come once or twice a year and they give the prison plenty of forewarning. So they paint, clean up, make sure everyone is squared away and go around yelling to all the prisoners to shut up and get off the doors. The inspectors only go where the prison directors lead them so they only see what the directors want them to see. They don't stop to talk to us, and if they did no one would make a complaint for fear of retaliation.

There needs to be realistic oversight and a system of checks and balances. Right now we are lucky to get one change of clean clothes a week. And it's so awful hot here in my cell. I haven't been given a clean tee shirt in two weeks, a clean towel in a month or a clean pillowcase in like three months. We're supposed to get all that every other day, and two clean sheets a week. But we only get one sheet and one set of boxers for the whole week.

This of course is against the rules and a lot of prisoners have written grievances, but still there are no changes.

Without air conditioning, especially in the Florida summer, imagine how you sweat day and night in one set of boxers all week. You can wash them in the sink but the bar of soap they give you will only last for one wash. By the time you turn them in they smell horrible, and so do the rest of your clothes. Then they overload the washer and use very little detergent, sometimes none when they run out.

But when the inspection people come once a year, they make sure they issue clean clothes, no holes or rips, and even come around asking what we need. So, you see, inspections are a joke, because they screw us all year until a day or two before they come. When they leave, it's back to business as usual.

I would also bring back the programs to help people leaving prison. They have paid their debt to society. They served their time. Unless they are sex offenders they shouldn't have to register. But instead, we all have to register. And it's hard enough to re-enter society and get a job when you're a convicted felon, but a convicted felon without skills?

So prison continues to be a revolving door. I don't think the government really wants to fix that. America has a prison economy. Look how many people are employed because of it, from the courthouse, judges, lawyers, janitors, police force, security guards, construction and the special industries that serve them. It's insane when you really think about it.

They need to bring back a few things to make serving time a little easier. I understand that prisons are not supposed to be fun, but now it's so tough, especially in Florida, that you have nothing to lose. Inmates are literally killing each other to get the death penalty. I know of three guys who have done it in the last four years. They even told the courts that's why they did it.

Same with the Department of Juvenile Justice. It was a joke as far as oversight went. They had QA, quality assurance. Again, the facilities knew before the inspectors came. People from other facilities came and checked on each other. You had your buddy checking on you so you will give them a good report because the next time they'll be checking on you. What a joke.

Solitary confinement for a kid? You lock up someone all day in a cell year after year and you best believe that it is going to mess them up mentally. They do it to thousands in prison every year in Florida, and they did it in juvenile prisons too. When the prisoners get out and do something crazy, what did you expect?

It's clear that solitary confinement causes mental illness, yet they use it for some very minor offenses. It should be used for only violent kids or adults, and even then they should be provided with something to keep them sane, like a television, radio, books, something that will connect them to other people.

The Department of Juvenile Justice should end privatization of juvenile prisons. The state has no business contracting out kids. These "programs" are trying to make a profit. That's their main goal, so they will cut too many corners. The Department of Children and Families has the same problems. If you are abused in a foster home and someone who works for the department is told, it is likely to be found not to be true. But if you had an outside source with no connection to the department, you might get a more fair and unbiased result, and the foster kid would be believed.

I wasn't believed when I was a foster kid, so I ran away, committed crimes, went to a juvenile prison and now I'm here. For life.

Prison Food; Redemption

Dear Sullivan,

God it's so hot in here. When the prisoners act up because of the heat, the guards punish us by turning off large fans in the walkways.

Your last letter was kind of weird. You asked for two totally different things. What kind of food do they give us, and what do I want as redemption for the murders I committed? It's easy to answer the first question, but I can hardly think of the second without getting really upset.

The "meat" we get here is basically all a soy product that looks good on paper because it's given different names, like "country patty, Salisbury steak, barbeque," but it's all the same. It's a patty that tastes like cardboard. We get some vegetables and bread and a cookie or cake for dessert. Also, they add water to anything they can to make it last longer, so that pudding is basically soup when it gets to you. Of course this is different when the outside inspectors come. Breakfast is a little better. We get pancakes or powdered eggs, grits and sometimes biscuits. Don't let the menu fool you. Pizza is really just cornbread mixed with some spaghetti sauce and maybe a little cheese thrown on top.

In November, I go back to see if I can make closed management three. If so, I'll be allowed contact visits so you won't have to worry about yelling through the glass. It will be a lot less crowded and you will be able to hear me.

Okay, I know I can't end without talking about redemption. It's easy to ask how can I do anything to redeem myself when I'm going to die in prison? Maybe that's a copout.

What I really want to say is that all that I've told you and written to you over the last seven or so years has been for redemption. Like I told you in the beginning, when you first wrote to me, was that I wanted to make sure that what happened to me never would happen to another foster kid anywhere. So I told you my story. I'm still so sorry that I killed those people.

But your book is my redemption. I hope it works.

One thing I do know for certain. The longer I'm here, the more I'm forgotten.

Leo

A Step Toward Redemption

"I'm not asking for forgiveness or pity. I just want to tell my story so that what happened to me never happens to another foster child again."

Leo Boatman

Leo Boatman has not read the book written about him. He will be angry to see the men he loves, but who exploited him, exposed for their sexual assaults and abuse. He did not want their secrets uncovered. These men are among only a few human beings who over the years continue to write him letters and visit him in prison. Understandably, Boatman has great fears these men will no longer visit or write after reading the book. By telling his story, Boatman prioritized the good that can come from the book over the risk of abandonment by his closest people. A step toward redemption by a killer.

Acknowledgments

I'm forever grateful to the late Ken Wooden—journalist, author and champion of children—who worked tirelessly to keep them from sexual abuse and out of juvenile prisons. Ken interviewed Leo Boatman in prison and contributed to this book. His perspective was invaluable. I am grateful to Dewey Caruthers, founder of the Caruthers Institute, a think tank for juvenile justice aimed at finding alternatives to incarceration. Dewey contributed to chapters on the mistakes the State of Florida made from Leo's birth through relative and foster care and his six years in juvenile prisons. I am grateful to Ben Montgomery, superb reporter for the St. Petersburg Times, who met Leo after writing his article about the arrest, which is part of this book. I am also grateful to my former juvenile court colleague and clinical psychologist, Dr. Adele Solazzo, who interviewed Leo in prison and gave me a frank assessment, which is part of this book. Without Ken, Dewey, Ben and Adele, this book wouldn't exist.

I next thank my former judicial assistant, Jerrilynn Evans, for her initial support of my pen pal relationship with Leo (although she bet me that he would never answer my first letter sent to him in prison!). Leo's sister Rose shared some important family information and I wish her well. Leo's godfather Greg tried to create a good relationship with Leo, and I'm grateful for his insights. Leo's court-appointed guardian ad litem, whom I've named Toby, I've been assured will never again be appointed a guardian ad litem for children in the State of Florida.

Many high school and college friends have encouraged me to continue this endeavor, for almost twenty years. Thanks, pals!

I thank my marvelous, very skilled editor, Denise McCabe, for making the manuscript readable, organized and timely.

Thanks to Alex Kale at Atmosphere Press. It was a pleasure to work with her.

Finally, I thank Leo Boatman, now sitting on death row, for sharing his life with me so that what happened to him never happens to another foster child again.

Many thanks to all.

Irene Sullivan

About Atmosphere Press

Founded in 2015, Atmosphere Press was built on the principles of Honesty, Transparency, Professionalism, Kindness, and Making Your Book Awesome. As an ethical and author-friendly hybrid press, we stay true to that founding mission today.

If you're a reader, enter our giveaway for a free book here:

SCAN TO ENTER
BOOK GIVEAWAY

If you're a writer, submit your manuscript for consideration here:

SCAN TO SUBMIT
MANUSCRIPT

And always feel free to visit Atmosphere Press and our authors online at atmospherepress.com. See you there soon!